I0157761

Early Praise for

RUPEE MILLIONAIRES

"Mr Kusy is clearly capable of writing vivid and enticing portraits of India – his past as a travel writer shines through, and we see India as if we are there first hand."

- Harper Collins reviewer

"A rip-roaring tale of dodgy dealings and hilarious happenings."

- Mark Roman, author, *The Ultimate Inferior Beings*

"A real snake charmer of a story."

- Terry Murphy, author, *Weekend in Weighton*

"India comes alive in the manner of such films as the Best Exotic Hotel Marigold. All the makings of a classic."

- Dee Harrison, author, *Firelord's Crown*

"Wonderfully encapsulates the vast, breathtaking country that is India. You feel you are there on the elephant's back."

- John Patrick, author, *Dropping Babies*

Also by Frank Kusy

Kevin and I in India
Off the Beaten Track: My Crazy Year in Asia
Ginger the Gangster Cat
Ginger the Buddha Cat

All titles available from Grinning Bandit Books

Rupee
Millionaires

Frank Kusy

First published in 2013 by

Grinning Bandit Books

http://grinningbandit.webnode.com

© Frank Kusy 2013

'Rupee Millionaires' is the copyright of Frank Kusy, 2013.

All rights reserved.

No part of this book may be reproduced or transmitted in any

form or by any means, electronic, digital or mechanical,

without permission in writing from the copyright owner.

ISBN 978-0-9575851-2-6

Cover design by Anna Donovan

DEDICATION

For my beloved mother...always in my heart.

Contents

Map	v
Epigraph	vii
Prologue	1
1. Here Comes Spud	3
2. On the Make	5
3. In The Beginning	9
4. Market Days	13
5. Life with Spud	20
6. Saree Wars	26
7. Special Requests	32
8. The Ups and Downs of Spud	41
9. What Makes a Rupee Millionaire?	50
10. Mister Bank-Rupert	58
11. Colourful Characters	66
12. Ram, Ram, the Camel Man	75
13. Recession? What Recession?	81
14. The Pushkar Posse	91
15. Susie	99
16. Troubles with Spud	106
17. Monsoon Madness	112
18. Spud vs Nita	121
19. Mister Order Cancel Man	131
20. Full Moon Camel Trek	140
21. Plague? What Plague?	147
22. Mother India	155
23. Margreet	162
24. Second Honeymoon	166
25. Mister Magic Trouser Man	173
26. Madge's 64-Million-Dollar Question	178
27. Busy Bobby	186
28. We Are the Agarwals	202
29. A "Poor Man's" Castle	210
30. Mister Duplicator	217
31. Thai-Tracked	221
32. A Very Bad Year	230
33. On being a Bad Buddhist	236
34. The Dark Side of Delhi	245
35. Burn Out	249
Postscript	258
Acknowledgements	260
About the author	261

Map

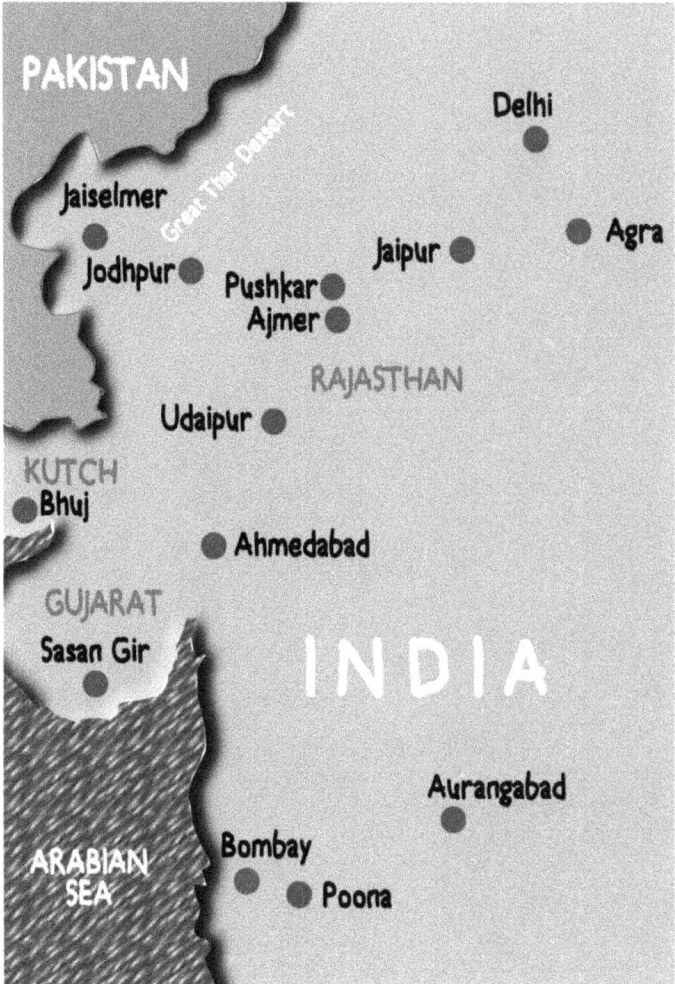

Epigraph

This is an (almost) true account of my life that was.

Some names have been changed to protect the innocent.

And some to protect myself against the not so innocent.

₹

Prologue

31 August 2011

Our anniversary lunch wasn't much compared to Will's and Kate's recent love-fest, but The Raj did a mean vindaloo. More importantly, we were happy. As Madge chatted to our usual waiter, I scanned the menu and came across 'Warped Chicken raped with Bacon'. I couldn't help smiling to myself. Indian restaurants and Indian menus always reminded me of my ill-fated quest to become a rupee millionaire. It seemed like a lifetime ago. For my ex-business partner Spud, it literally was a lifetime ago. It finished him off – just before he could finish me off.

Sometimes, not often, I could think of Spud and forget the anger and heartache and misery. Sometimes I could feel the tiniest pang of guilt at his squalid demise. And sometimes, like when reading the menu in *The Raj*, I would be reminded of a funny memory of Spud. Like the time he ordered bacon – no, it was sausages, wasn't it? – in a vegetarian town called Pushkar.

But more often my mind was flooded with less funny memories, like the night he forced a Muslim tailor to eat mutton curry at Ramadan, doing his best to invite an international fatwa on the both of us. Yes, the bad memories dominated – the abuse, the mental torture, the drug plants and the many death threats. There was no doubt about it, I was

1

much better off without that bald little menace.

Having pushed all the bitter memories to the back of my mind – and enjoyed a few *Tiger* beers – I was feeling quite content by the time I arrived home. Madge had gone to pop the kettle on and I switched on the TV. Settling in for a quiet afternoon snooze, I stretched absent-mindedly across the settee and closed my eyes.

Then the phone rang.

It was my old friend and customer, Sharon in Poole, and what she said took my breath away.

'You'll never guess who just walked into my shop!' she gushed. *'Spud!'*

'WHAT?'

'Yes, it really was him. He's not dead at all. He's been entertaining Her Majesty in Wandsworth for the past 12 years. He blew up the wrong house – one with a policeman in it.'

'What did he *say?*'

'Not a lot. Except that he's heard you're writing a book about him. And he wanted me to pass on a short one-word message.'

'Which is?'

'"Don't."'

*

What follows is the full story of what Spud doesn't want you to know...

₹

Chapter 1

Here Comes Spud

Spud was under his table when the Petrovs showed up. The two of them, Ivan and Sergei, had strolled in, squinting curiously at my market stall. They seemed particularly interested in all the silk clothing I had just brought back from India.

Ivan—the tall, dark, handsome one—was relatively polite. He waved a slender hand at his own stall, packed with the very same silk, and said, 'I think we have a problem.'

Viktor—his short, psychotic brother—was more to the point. The stubby fingers of one hand curled around my table, lifted it and tipped the whole thing over. He glared at me. 'If that goes back up,' he growled, 'I'm going to petrol-bomb it.'

I had heard enough of Viktor to know I should take the threat seriously. According to Spud, Viktor had already dispatched two silk competitors that morning – one by holding him against a wall and punching him repeatedly in the head. So I gestured over my shoulder with one thumb. 'Have you met my new partner?' I asked. 'He'll want to know what you have to say about silk, too.'

Viktor might have been a psycho, but he knew a worse psycho when he saw one. Spud, resplendent in his best lunatic grin and a pair of wraparound reflecting sunglasses, reared up from under his table like a demented bulldog. He said nothing. He didn't need to. He just stood there, rocking dangerously back and forth on his heels, until Viktor took a step backwards, breaking the stand-off. Ivan crouched, gingerly helping to set the stall back up, and a tacit agreement was reached: the Petrovs would move their pitch up the road to Covent Garden, and I would stay put in St Martin-in-the-Fields.

I had made a deal with the Devil, entering into this partnership with Spud, but I really hadn't had any other choice. All in all, it worked out well. On the one hand, Spud was very good at scaring people, a talent which occasionally came in handy. On the other, he was funny, surprisingly intelligent, and full of big plans for the future.

The following morning, Spud appeared with a huge pile of scaffolding and wordlessly welded our two stalls together. This was his idea of a partnership: no formal paperwork, just a brief handshake and a hastily combined double pitch. The day after that, now that we had a much larger area in which to operate, we brought in £500 in silk clothing alone.

₹

Chapter 2

On the Make

The one miracle of my life before India was that I never got arrested.

Back then I was known as 'dodgy' Frank Kusy. Most people took in my beaten-up leather jacket, dusty trilby hat, and dishevelled, greying beard and incorrectly assumed that I was a drug dealer. I suppose my round Lennon spectacles and the permanently abstracted expression I wore behind them did nothing to dispel the theory.

The truth was that I didn't just look weird. I *was* weird. And with my kind of background, that was hardly surprising. I lost my father when I was two, which left my Hungarian mother and me to survive on the breadline. She and I lived in one shared room in the poorest section of London. My mother worked all day—and all night too, darning dresses – so she could keep a leaking roof over our heads.

I wasn't given pocket money, so I learned to earn my own. My first enterprise consisted of prising up the floorboards in our house so I could retrieve the gas meter shillings that had slipped through the cracks. Then I traded rare pennies with geeks in mackintoshes. Later on, shortly after entering primary school, I began sneaking into big auction houses in The Strand

and bidding for collectable stamps. I hung around the doors, watching the crowds, then gained entrance by grabbing old geezers' hands and flashing pleading eyes up at them.

'I want to buy some stamps,' I said, 'but they won't let me because I'm not old enough. Can I be your son for the day?' They never refused.

I was determined not to be poor. By the age of seven I made homemade fireworks and sold them to friends, then stashed the profits up the chimney. My mother became acquainted with all the local firemen; they knew exactly where to come when a neighbourhood kid blew up a pile of dog poo or some hapless garden shed. They didn't seem to mind coming. In fact, more than one of those heroes asked her out. With her perfect smile, perfect figure, and perfect pile of jet black hair, she looked just like Jackie Onassis.

When I was eight, I got my first taste of market trading. Every Saturday morning I cycled down to Whitechapel to help an old cockney called Charlie on his second-hand book stall. Though this job didn't last long.

'He's a very nice man, is Charlie,' I told my mother. 'And he's generous, too. Everyone in the market keeps giving him money, but he doesn't keep it. He gives it to another nice man called Ronnie Kray. Ronnie says he's there to protect them all!'

My mother promptly confiscated my bicycle.

When I entered my teens, my budding career as a pint-sized wheeler-dealer came to an abrupt end. I was packed off to a north London Jesuit school, where grim, black-cowled priests took pride in crushing my natural exuberance. My mother had expected me to receive the best education in the world at that school. What I received instead was daily punishments meted out with a leathered whalebone.

The priests disliked more than my stubborn resistance to male authority. They disapproved of just about everything about me. I was a tall, geeky boy and stuck out like a sore thumb in the playground. As a result, I was the first to be picked out for any disturbance. Maybe it was a poor decision on my part, but I hung around with the two worst kids in the school, who were later expelled for flushing a holy crucifix down the toilet. Those were the kind of boys I used as role models. To the priests I seemed hell-bent on creating trouble. I suppose they were correct to a degree. It's true I was curious to see how far I could provoke these zealot priests until they lost their sanctimonious cool. And I was, admittedly, a very precocious child. I enjoyed asking awkward, rhetorical questions like, 'How many angels *do* dance on the head of a pin?'

But it didn't seem to matter that some events occurred over which I had no control—after all, how could I have known my voice would break when they put me in the choir during the ordination of nine priests?

Their punishments made me devious. I held pretend fainting fits, I invented complicated alibis, I even feigned total memory loss. The lies got so bad that I had a recurring nightmare that I was Pinocchio, and my nose was permanently circling the globe.

On one occasion, when things got completely out of hand, I invented Wojciech. Wojciech was my identical twin brother, and he was visiting from Hungary.

'We know it was you who blew up that tree that fell on number 26 and destroyed the roof,' accused a police officer. 'We have six eye witnesses.'

'Nem tudom,' I replied, shaking my head with innocence. 'My name Wojciech. No understand.'

'Your name is Frank Kusy,' insisted the officer. 'And we have you bang to rights.'

I nodded, letting comprehension brighten my expression. *'Cusunum,* thank you. My twin brother, Frank, he is very bad boy. I tell him so, write him long letter. He go Budapest.'

The policeman scratched his head and left, bemused.

My poor mother. Every Parent's Day she would troop to my school in the dwindling hope of good news, only to be sent home crying by some teacher who thought I should see a psychiatrist.

At seventeen, I cut a deal with her. She agreed to write a letter to the school saying I was suffering from nervous exhaustion. In return I would apply myself to my studies at home. The arrangement worked. Blessed with fierce concentration and a near-photographic memory, I learnt one-third of the entire syllabus in six weeks. I passed my A levels with straight As. Lucky for me, the questions came from the right one-third!

As soon as I reached university, I dropped Catholicism, deciding to take up astrology and Steiner philosophy instead. These paths were, I knew, only clues to destiny – they had no power to change it – but they were infinitely better than the world of pain and cruelty I had left behind.

My twenties was a decade I prefer to forget. I moved from one dead-end job to another, working with insurance, sales, publishing, and social work. Not one of these jobs lasted more than a few months.

It wasn't until I turned thirty and discovered both Buddhism and India that I latched onto a faith and a country that suited me perfectly. Together they gave me the freedom and the constant inner challenge I craved, along with a growing sense of purpose.

₹

Chapter 3

In The Beginning

What I liked about Buddhism—well, the version of Buddhism which I chose, anyway—was the absence of guilt, hellfire, priests, and temples. Oh, and the lack of rules and regulations. Apparently everything was okay as long as I respected life: my own as well as everyone else's.

Best of all, I was allowed to chant for money.

One of the Buddhists in my area had a helicopter. I wanted one of those.

I also wanted that elusive thing called 'enlightenment.' I'd tried yoga but had concussed myself falling backwards from one of the more complicated positions. I'd tried transcendental meditation, but the concept had been lost on me. I worked myself up to near-hysteria trying to free my mind of all thoughts.

I was told that if I chanted the title of the *Lotus Sutra*, the Buddha's most important teaching, I would achieve enlightenment as a matter of course – no counting of breaths, no sitting in uncomfortable poses, no boring 'emptying of the mind.' Just a simple *Nam-myoho-renge-kyo*. What could be easier?

My mother, a hard-line Catholic, was not impressed by my

new choice of religion. 'Jesus died to redeem our sins,' she scolded me. 'How can you abandon Him?'

'I haven't got a problem with Jesus,' I replied, still sulking in my thirties. 'Just all those priests He keeps employing!'

My new mentor, Dick Causton, was a whole lot better than a priest. He had graduated from being a colonel in the army to becoming the leader of our small Nichiren sect in the U.K. Tall, dignified, and charismatic, Dick reminded me of a white Morgan Freeman. He was the first male figure to gain my undivided respect.

That's who I want to be when I'm seventy, I decided. *This is the Buddhism for me!*

Dick set me on the path to India. 'So you want to see where this great religion began?' he asked, raising his arms as if to encompass the world. 'Well, go out there and be like a sponge. Soak it all up. Then, when you get back, squeeze it all out. Produce something remarkable!'

India was fun. It took me two or three trips to really pick up on that, but as I did so, I found that the childlike quality of the country – the simple curiosity, the warm-hearted openness, the sheer craziness of it – struck a chord in me. Six weeks into my first trip, around February of 1985, I had forgotten that I had ever worn a suit to work. By the time I returned in April, I had vowed never to work again. Somehow, I determined, I would be going back to India on a regular basis – and that was when I started to write.

Dick had said I should squeeze out the sponge of my travels, then produce something of value with whatever came out. I decided to use my experiences to write a book about the real India, a serious accounting of its poverty, politics, and religion. But the real India was far more surreal than serious. It was like a giant playground wherein everything—people, traffic, and livestock—bounced off each other at random.

I had attempted to put pen to paper before, but I'd never got past the first three chapters. I'd simply lacked the incentive to go any further. Now I had all the incentive in the world. It was either getting paid to write about India or return to the drudgery of running an old people's home in Clapham.

So, discarding the idea of writing a 'serious' book, I decided instead to type up the diary of my first trip through India. When I'd finished I packaged it up, then sent it off to forty-two publishers and agents. Then I hopped on a plane to Japan, spending every penny I had, and prayed to the main Buddhist temple that my gamble would succeed.

I returned to London with the worst case of flu I'd ever had. On the positive side, the phones started ringing. The first call was from a minor publisher who wanted my book. The second was from a bigger publisher who wanted me to write a travel guide to the whole of India. It was a dream come true. The money they offered wasn't much—£2500 advance and 7.5% of royalties on sales—but all my flights were paid for, and they threw in lots of free hotels. Suddenly I was doing what I'd always wanted to do: travel and write. My life, which had been on hold until this moment, finally began to move forward.

From this point on, I began to lead a split existence – half the year in India, the other half in England writing *about* India. And each time I came home, with a bagful of notes and tapes to transcribe, I carried more of India back with me. I felt lighter, freer, more at ease with myself. India was rubbing off on me, I realised, and when I laughed now, it was not shy and restrained as before, but loud and contagious – a true reflection of what I felt about myself and about India: that both things were so wacky, so absurd, that I just *had* to laugh.

Four years on, and I had written guides to not just India, but half of Asia too. I was now 35, and my mother was putting pressure on me to 'get a proper job', since I had never had more than £400 in the bank. That was when the business thing, the market stall, happened.

And it happened in the most peculiar way.

₹

Chapter 4

Market Days

It was a warm spring day in 1989, and I was sitting on the lawn of the Megh Niwas Hotel in Jaipur, talking to my old friend, Colonel Fateh Singh, the genial proprietor. I had been introduced to the Colonel a few years before by "Bubbles", the Maharajah of Jodhpur. The three of us had played nine holes of golf out in the desert, each shot played off a small, square piece of green lawn produced from Bubbles's filing cabinet. Tall, balding, and irrepressibly jovial, Fateh had brought two bottles of whisky along with his golf clubs. None of us finished the game.

I was telling the Colonel about my very first day in India in 1985. I had been stuck on a traffic island in the middle of a busy Delhi thoroughfare, too scared to cross the road. Out of nowhere appeared a thin, dapper little Sikh dressed in an immaculate black suit and carrying a matching sleek briefcase. He looked me up and down, then, with no preamble at all, politely enquired:

'And sir, what is your purpose in life?'

I hadn't known what to say, so just stuttered, 'Erm … to cross the road?'

Hearing this, my new 'friend' grabbed my arm and ushered

me, like a tiny turbaned sat-nav, through the maelstrom of traffic until we reached the other side. From there I walked alone to the safety of my digs at the YMCA, considering the little man's words with every step.

'The whole way back,' I told the Colonel, 'I kept asking myself, "What *is* my purpose in life? What *am* I doing here?" You see, I came to India with one idea: to check out the birthplace of Buddhism. But right from the get-go, all everyone wanted was either to buy my watch and walkman, or to sell me something!'

The Colonel laughed, eyes twinkling. 'Yes, we Indians like to do business. It is in our blood. It is the key to our soul. You should try business, Frank! It would be a most spiritual experience!'

That is how it started. One minute I was a struggling travel writer with five guides in print but not enough money to pay the rent. In the next I was checking out semi-precious stones with the Colonel in Jaipur's seedy Johari Bazar.

'Buy my packet! Buy my packet!' shouted a throng of grimy gem cutters, climbing over themselves to sell me stones they had smuggled out in their mouths or under their armpits during their lunch breaks.

I was mesmerised. 'What a buzz!' I shouted to the Colonel. 'Spiritual or not, I was *born* to do this!'

I couldn't have set up shop at a better time. It was the start of the yuppie '90s, and Maggie Thatcher was encouraging new businesses through her popular Enterprise Allowance Scheme. I applied for it without much hope—after all, I looked like a hippy and my work c.v. was one long catalogue of disaster— but I figured it was worth a shot. In my experience, when I really wanted something, I always performed well. So I got a haircut, shook the mothballs out of my one and only suit, and spoke like a toff to the powers-that-be. It worked. I was given a bank loan of £3000 and a weekly stipend of £40 to get myself going. And I spent it all on silver jewellery handpicked by the Colonel in India. Six months down the line, when the Scheme called me into its offices to see how I was doing, I brought the whole place to a standstill by selling trinkets hand-over-fist to bored secretaries. That was when I knew I had it made.

Shy and solitary by nature, I blossomed as a market trader. I had my mother to thank for that. She didn't approve of my new vocation ('You don't want to be a barrow boy all your life!') or my repeated visits to India ('What's with the earring and the hippy scarf?') or my girlfriends ('Where did you find this one—on a beach in Goa?'), but while she was short on praise, she was unstinting in her support, no matter what I decided to do.

So it was, one wintry day in 1989, that she helped set up my very first market stall in St Martin's. It didn't look like much at first—a bare 6 x 4 table with a rainproof awning—but she waved me out of the way and quickly arranged it into something reminiscent of an oriental boudoir. She set a neat pile of exotic cushions in one corner and a tempting array of glittering jewellery in the other, then hung a colourful portrait of a Chinese dragon as a striking backdrop. I stood timidly behind the table as she set things in motion, storming into the stream of pedestrians and tackling passers-by. I watched in silent awe as she stopped them dead in their tracks, barraging them with stream-of-consciousness inquisitions about their lives, hopes, and dreams, generally making them feel like the most important people on God's earth.

Her charm was irresistible. Nobody she spoke to ever left without buying something, and by the end of the day the stall was virtually empty. It had been amazing, seeing her in action, like watching a hypnotist at work. And what she taught me was this: you can sell anyone just about anything *if* you talk long enough, and *if* you take a real interest in their lives.

My mother was entirely wasted as a housewife. She should have been an estate agent or a stockbroker.

My first year was a grind. I had never really lost the tall, thin physique which had attracted so much negative attention back in school, and with this new business enterprise I grew leaner still. Even my hair thinned, so I took to wearing a bandana. But I was determined. I travelled to India six times that year, doubling my stock on each occasion and lugging everything home by hand. On my final visit I gambled everything I had on a good Christmas and ended up overextending myself, turning up at Delhi airport with no fewer than seventeen suitcases of clothes, crafts, and jewellery. I stared at the bags, almost overwhelmed with despair. *I'll never get this lot through!* I despaired, but then the Air India check-in lady beckoned me over.

'Are you on this flight?' she enquired. When I nodded unhappily she asked, 'How many bags do you have?'

I pointed at the three bags standing in plain sight, then— very reluctantly—indicated the long line of bags placed strategically out of sight. She asked what they contained, and I lied. I said they belonged to a sick girlfriend in a Delhi hotel, and they contained rock samples for her forthcoming archaeological project.

Her expression brightened. 'Well, you are fortunate!' she exclaimed. 'Today is *lucky* day, the festival of our Independence!' She gave a complicit wink, labelled all seventeen bags "Fragile", and sent them through.

My gamble paid off. Every other vendor in the market had

bought stock from London wholesalers, forcing them to charge a lot more for their merchandise. Not one had been able to compete with my prices. Having made no profit all year long, I found myself on Christmas Eve with £10,000 in my pockets. I had worked, slept, and breathed on my stall for three weeks solid, leaving me tired but triumphant.

Life on a market stall was however no picnic. Even I had my good days and my bad days. And for every good day— when I might sell a £100 bedspread or a £50 marble chess-set—there were far more bad days. Days when it rained down in sheets and I sold one backpack for £5, not even enough to cover the rent of my table. Getting up every morning at 6am was yet another drag. Sometimes I was so tired that by the time I'd finished putting up my stall, it was time to start taking it all down again. Then there were the customers, who ranged from the kind and enthusiastic to the downright tedious. The *most* tedious, in my experience, were the beach freaks from Goa who lit up bongs on my stall and complained about the price of my nose studs.

'One pound for a *nose stud?* they whined. 'What a *rip-off*, man! They only cost ten pee in Goa!'

'Go back to Goa then!' I snarled in reply. 'And put that pipe away. We're not in India!'

I got ripped off from time to time, too. One enthusiastic woman with a shop in Bournemouth liked my Tibetan bone bracelets so much she ordered eight hundred of them. It was only after I'd lugged them all the way home from Delhi that she decided to buy only fifty, saying she'd take the rest 'later on.'

At first I was distraught, having so much money tied up in unwanted trinkets, but I soon turned the situation to my advantage. I displayed a single bracelet on my table and placed a "Not for Sale" sticker on it. The next day a busload of American students turned up and were drawn like iron filings to a magnet. When they asked why the bracelet was not for sale, I shrugged with apology.

'It's my lucky bracelet,' I told them. 'It's been personally blessed by the Dalai Lama, and it protects my stall. I couldn't possibly sell it.'

Of course after that, they all wanted one—at any price. I waited until the bidding went crazy, then I sighed with dramatic resignation. 'Come back tomorrow,' I said. 'There's a Tibetan lama in town, and he might have some more for sale.'

Come back they did, and I offloaded one hundred bracelets in an hour—at 20 dollars apiece. In the weeks that followed, word got around. Further busloads of Americans arrived, and all seven hundred and fifty bracelets were snapped up. I made a real killing on that one. And when the shop lady from Bournemouth rang up for the rest of her order—some six months later—I cheerily informed her, 'They're all gone. *So* sorry!'

It may not have been entirely ethical, but I didn't feel bad about telling the odd 'story.' As long as my customers were happy, I didn't see anything wrong with stretching the truth to make a sale. Besides, there were plenty of other traders around with far fewer scruples—and far sharper teeth. Ruthless traders like the Petrovs who were looking way beyond St Martin's to expand their businesses. A new decade was dawning, and as London's banks and stock markets started filling with young entrepreneurs known as 'yuppies,' a completely different kind of wheeler-dealer – the world traveller merchant adventurer – was emerging on the other side of the world, in India.

At the end of 1990 the tiny dot in the Rajasthan desert that had been Pushkar suddenly became the small business hub of the Asian world. No one knew why it happened or who started it, but this once sleepy hippy resort, my favourite place in all India, began trucking in vast quantities of second-hand sarees from Bombay and making them into cheap, funky clothing. The profit margins, for anyone with a market stall or a shop back in the West, were *huge* and traders from all over – the US, Canada, Germany, Israel and France – were soon pouring in to place large orders. The whole town was instantly transformed into a Mecca of multi-national mass production and the so-called 'saree wars' of 1991/92 kicked off.

₹

Chapter 5

Life with Spud

I knew I was onto a good thing when I put my first rail of silk tops out for sale. The refashioned sarees had cost me twenty pence each, and they all flew off my table in one day for £5 apiece. I couldn't believe it. A quick mental calculation showed 2000 per cent profit on each top. I immediately booked a flight back to India.

Then my luck ran out. When I returned to my market a week later, six large cases of silk in tow, I discovered it wasn't my market anymore. The Petrovs were in town and so was their silk. There was also a new guy on the stall next to me, selling jewellery. This was Spud. And the very first words Spud said to me were, 'I think you're screwed, mate. You need a partner.'

I shook my head. 'No thanks.' After all, I was doing just fine on my own.

At the same time, I couldn't help but be intrigued by my new neighbour. The guy appeared to be totally fearless. And for some reason I couldn't fathom, he spent more time under his table, polishing his silver and sorting out stock, than above it. In fact, he only surfaced when he heard a customer approach—rather like a small, hairy spider, hiding in wait for his prey. The only place he was *not* hairy, I noted with amusement, was his head, which was entirely bald. His whole appearance was such that when he did pop out from under his table, anyone who happened to be standing there was panicked into an immediate purchase.

'Competition is good,' declared Spud, and he knew what he was talking about. Every day or so, shortly after facing down Viktor, Spud strolled up to Ivan's stall in Covent Garden and checked out his prices, which rose all the time. A silk saree dress, for instance, shot up from £7 to £15 in just one week. Spud adjusted his prices accordingly, and everybody was happy. The only person not happy was the taxman, who saw hardly any of the profits. Ironically, the enterprise allowance scheme Ms. Thatcher had set up the likes of Spud and me had failed to account for one thing: market traders, unlike shops, had no cash tills to ring through sales. Most of the money we made went straight into our pockets.

It didn't stay there long, though. At Spud's insistence nearly all of it went straight back into stock. 'Stock is *power*!' stated Spud importantly, and he gutted his whole house to accommodate it. He then handed me three grand—his half of our initial investment—and sent me straight back to India to buy as much silk as possible.

Spud wanted to become a rupee millionaire. He figured that if he had a million rupees—about £20,000—everyone would forget he was a small, fat, bald plumber from Peckham, and scores of nubile women would flock to his cash and shag him senseless.

One can tell a lot about a man by his heroes. Spud's heroes were John Belushi, Suggs from "Madness" and, in particular, Alexei Sayle. That's right – three crazy comedians. But Spud wasn't actually crazy. He was just crazed. That's why I took him on as a partner. Nobody messed with Spud, not even vegetarians. A hard-line vegetarian appeared at his stall one day and pointed with disgust, at the stream of oily burger grease running down his chin.

'Uuurr!' she complained. 'Don't you know that meat is murder?'

'Meat may be murder,' he snapped back, shoving the burger in her face, 'but veg is *TOR-TURE*!'

*

I heard later that Spud's sister, who had bequeathed him her stall, advised him against going into partnership with me.

'That Frank is a lone wolf,' she cautioned her brother. 'I don't think he does partners.'

But Spud thought otherwise. In the short while before the Petrovs showed up, he had watched me at work and had been impressed.

'This guy is like a crocodile,' he'd told someone. 'He sleepwalks his way into work, lures his customers to his table with inconsequential chatter, then snap! He suddenly wakes up to make that crucial sale. I could use him!'

On the surface, Spud and I were the original odd couple: one small, brash, and belligerent; the other tall, polite, and absent-minded. We were in fact such polar opposites, both physically and temperamentally, that nobody thought we could work together.

But work together we did. In later years, when I saw a film called *The Big Lebowski*, I would recognize myself in the 'Dude' – calm, laidback, empathic – and Spud in the Dude's best friend, Walter – violently proactive, anal, socially dysfunctional. In short, although we couldn't have been more different, Spud and I perfectly complemented each other. When style and tact were required, I stepped in. When threats and bullying were called for, it was Spud's turn. It was, in effect, the ideal business marriage.

At least...to start with.

My only criticism of Spud, apart from his talent for crashing into people's lives, was that Spud didn't want my friendship. He enjoyed my company well enough, respected my ability to get things done through charm and humour, but he held me at arm's length. I, on the other hand, was interested in just about *everybody*. Sure, that was partly because being personable sold more stuff, but deep down, the main reason was that I wanted everybody to like me. Ultra-sensitive and raised on criticism, I made a point of doing everything possible to put other people at their ease using praise, flattery, and compliments.

It was difficult for me to accept Spud's rejection of friendship, but the problem was entirely his. He was emotionally shut down. Not even once did he ask, 'How are you?' or 'Can I be of help?' And it wasn't just with me. He didn't seem interested in anybody, which is why I found Spud, the ultimate social nightmare, so baffling. How could he block out the rest of humanity and be such a moon-blank face, when I could not imagine stepping out my front door without greeting the neighbours?

By the end of our first week together, I had all but given up on solving the mystery of Spud. Imagine my surprise then when a short, chubby lady turned up at my stall one day, asking for Spud.

'I'm Lou, his ex-wife,' she informed me, 'and I've come for my divorce settlement.'

I looked her up and down, and decided that she looked

exactly *like* Spud, but with a yellow wig. 'He's out to lunch,' I
replied, 'but can I be of help? I'm his new partner.'

Lou made to leave, then turned back. 'It's none of my
business,' she said quietly, 'but do you know what you're
getting yourself into? I spent two years with that nutter. The
minute we got married he turned all cold and hostile on me.
All I wanted was kids, and he kept putting me off, saying,
"You're too fat, girl! Lose some weight!" *Me* fat!' She blew a
dismissive snort through her nose. 'He should've looked in the
mirror! Give him a message, will you? Tell him I'm over the
disease he brought home from that prostitute, thanks very
much, and I've got a kid by a new man now. So cough up
some cash, or I'm taking him to court!'

I felt sorry for Lou and confronted Spud with her demands,
but he just laughed. 'She'll be lucky. I'm not paying that bitch
a red cent!'

One thing about me bothered Spud, and he made sure I
knew it. He didn't like being hugged. This was bad for him
since I—the only child of a doting mother—was used to
hugging *everything*, be it human, animal, or invertebrate. Spud
didn't mind this tactile bonhomie when it came to our
customers – they seemed to *love* being cuddled and called
'darlin' and 'pet' and 'mate' all the time, so it was good for
business – but he himself hated it. He hated even being
touched, Lou told me later. Nobody in *his* family had hugged
each other. It was a sissy thing, a weakness, and he had only
got this far in life (apparently) by *not* hugging anyone. Once,
and only once, I'd tried to get close, saying: 'Don't you want
to be friends then?' And Spud had snapped back: 'Fuck off! I
don't want to be "known". I want to be an *enigma*!' The
hugging stopped.

*

This did not, however, stop me admiring Spud. I particularly admired Spud's ferocious energy, the way he just kept on going, like an everlasting battery, until he suddenly dropped from exhaustion. Spud could go four days, sometimes five, with no sleep at all, and all the time – while the rest of planet Earth was happily snoozing – he was *doing* something. He was either dreaming up big plans for world domination, or he was ringing me at 3am to tell me about them. At other times, he was dashing to and fro like a Duracell bunny – sorting out stock, doing complex figure-work, and tinkering around with our market stall. In short, he was totally wired.

Up until his ex-wife's appearance, I hadn't really known much about Spud's personality, other than that which he'd shown me. On impulse, I rang up Lou to satisfy my curiosity.

'I'm sorry about the money, and I hope you don't mind my calling,' I said, 'but I have a question. I don't know why you should tell a virtual stranger this, but now you've got me worried. What *does* make this man tick?'

Lou gave a hollow laugh. 'Oh, that's easy. He's not right in the head. Anyone who can get discharged from the army for "unreasonable conduct" has a screw loose. He was also a raging alcoholic until the time I met him.'

'What's the reason for it?'

She shrugged. 'He's the youngest and smallest of eleven kids from Ireland. Because of that he's always had a lot to prove and a good reason to think big. That's why he's so *driven!*'

What she said made a lot of sense in terms of his personality. What I couldn't figure out was why Spud, so obviously tight with money, had trusted me with every penny he had. I could have just run off with it.

As it was, maybe I should have.

₹

Chapter 6

Saree Wars

On the 29th of March 1990, I landed in Delhi – and straight into trouble.

'Get out of the car,' the policeman ordered, pointing a gun through the taxi window. 'Get out of the car now!'

We'd stopped at a dark, desolate checkpoint in the middle of nowhere, half an hour out of Delhi airport, and I was about to be fleeced by three corrupt Sikh policemen. There was no way I was going to get out of that car. In addition to the £6,000 I was legally entitled to bring into India (the joint 'partnership' money) I was carrying £10,000 of "excess" foreign currency within two hidden armband wallets. This illegal excess was to pay off past loans from Indian suppliers. If I stepped out of the vehicle, I would lose it all.

I had three choices: be brave, be stupid, or select that mad, impetuous place in between. Staring into the barrel of the gun, I made my decision.

'What do you want?' I politely enquired.

'Get out of the car!' repeated the policeman. 'I want to see your papers!'

'Okay,' I said, handing him my press card. 'And I want to see your badge. I am a travel writer, I am going to the Oberoi

Maidens hotel, and I am seeing your police chief in the morning for breakfast. Please give me your badge number as well as those of your two colleagues.'

The gun wavered, but stayed in place. 'Why is this?' demanded the Sikh.

I gifted him with the warmest of smiles. 'Because you are such good friends to foreign tourists, I would like to recommend all three of you for promotion!'

The gun promptly dropped and was replaced by a salute. 'Please tell Inspector Singh,' the man stuttered, 'that we are honoured to welcome the Press!'

I waited until we were safely on our way again then leant forward to berate my taxi driver. 'Why did you take me to this bad place?' I accused him. 'And why do you let bad policemen steal from people like me?'

The driver shrugged, resignation clear in the sag of his shoulders. 'If I no stop there,' he said, 'they take away my licence!'

This was obviously a well-practiced scam, and I was vaguely proud of myself for getting past it so easily. I had no reason to expect it to happen again.

I was so naïve.

Six months later I was back at Delhi airport, this time with Spud, who I'd already told about my close-shave story. Suitably enthralled, he decided to bring along his camcorder in case there was a repeat performance. To Spud's delight, we were back at the same checkpoint half an hour out of the airport, staring into the barrel of the same police gun. I couldn't believe it. I also couldn't believe that Spud was scrabbling about in the back of the taxi, ready to poke his camcorder through the half-open window.

'Put that *away!*' I hissed. 'If they see you filming them,

we're as good as dead!'

Spud sulked, the Sikh looked in and recognised me, the salute went back up, and we were on our way again.

This was Spud's first experience of India, and it taught me one thing: if you take on a loose cannon as a partner, you have to be careful it doesn't blow up in your face.

The next day, as Saddam Hussein stormed into Kuwait, Spud and I wandered into Delhi. And the first thing we did was get on an elephant. One minute it was parked by the side of the road; the next we had hopped on board at the invitation of the driver and were swaying down Delhi's busiest thoroughfare, Main Bazar.

'This is the bollocks!' enthused Spud. 'I mean, when you're on top of an elephant, you are the *business*, you are the *man!*' From where I sat behind him I was treated to the sight of his bald head swinging back and forth, following the lines of people on either side of us. 'Everybody else is down there somewhere, and they're all scurrying out of our way!'

It was fun having someone else around, I decided. Having experienced India so many times on my own, I was in danger of becoming jaded with the place. Now, seeing it fresh through Spud's eyes, I began to recapture the feelings of awe and excitement with which I had first viewed the country. In particular, the feeling of being an alien suddenly dropped onto a distant planet.

'I can't get my head around it,' Spud said, keeping a firm grip on the saddle. 'As soon as you get over here, everyone is operating under a completely different set of rules. All of a sudden you're on Mars and walking down the high street. When someone comes up and starts to hassle you, how do you behave?' He barked out a laugh. 'Who knows? Do you smack them in the head or smile and give them money? Everything you've been conditioned to do, right down the years, is absolutely useless!'

I nodded silent agreement, and from my vantage point on top of the elephant, noticed something I hadn't seen before: the whole long, straggling road that was Main Bazar was criss-crossed with a spidery confusion of overhead wires. It looked like someone had got hold of all the electricity cables and patched them together in motley order, so as to provide every shop with a light, a telephone, and a TV. The general effect was of a frontier shantytown where there were no rules or regulations, and no one had any fear of either being electrocuted or of buildings falling down around them. Everything—from the cows and dogs to the scooters and wedding processions—moved in slow motion, all of them complaining in loud barks, trumpets, horns, and tannoys, creating a twenty-four hour cacophony of noise and brouhaha.

'Forget St Martin's!' I shouted to Spud. 'This is the market to end all markets! It runs for six days a week, and on Mondays—the one day it is supposed to be closed—it's still open!'

I shut my eyes and inhaled the pungent aromas of stale piss, rotting fruit, dung, and decay, over-laden (just) by the sweet fragrances of rose, sandalwood, and frangipani. It was a heady, intoxicating mix and could belong to only one country: India. My ears welcomed the distinct sounds: the jingling bicycle bells, the hooting rickshaws, the blaring taxis, and the collective roar of a thousand voices shouting at the same time. Bullock drivers demanded space, Indian housewives bargained over vegetables, touts and moneychangers haggled with tourists, and every few seconds someone wandered up to enquire, 'Hashish? What you want? Anything possible, Mister. Change dollar? You remember me? Wot is my nem? What country you? Why you no speak me? You no like India? Why not?'

The syrup of India flowed over and around me, and I became one with the din and the smells, absorbed into the vast, heaving melting pot that was Main Bazar. Overhead, far beyond the impossible spaghetti junction of cables and wiring, scores of wild kites soared in ever-widening circles, their distant shrieks faint over the honk and blare of the traffic below.

'It's mad, it's bad, and very, very real,' I informed Spud, leaning in to yell in his ear. 'No escape possible, and right in your face!'

I loved Main Bazar. It was street-life as street-life was meant to be. Halfway down the market I spied three cows facing the shop window of a jeweller's. The owner couldn't shoo them away ('holy' cow!) so they just stood there, a trio of static cattle, looking as if they were choosing a gift for a friend but unable to make up their minds. Further down hunched the dogs, so sad that deep furrows cut between their big brown eyes, so desperate for affection they cuddled up to anything—including vagrant calves or parked motorbikes—just to find a "friend." Many had only three legs and were hopping around with care, trying to avoid losing another.

'I call them the haunted hounds of Paharganj,' I told Spud when he pointed at them, 'because I've never seen any animals look so very, very worried.'

At the top of the market we stopped the elephant, climbed down, and went walkabout. Our first stop was an old print shop where we bought two ancient business cards. I became 'Babu Baloo: King of Melodies' and invaded roadside shops, singing bad pop songs and begging for money. Spud became 'Ashok Singh: The President's Bodyguard' and darted around various passers-by, pretending to protect them from imaginary attackers. Later on, we donned the clobber we'd nicked from our Thai Airways flight, wrapped lilac pillowcases and blankets over our heads and shoulders, and tucked royal orchids behind our ears. Then we wandered around, telling everyone who asked that we were Thai Airways Buddhists.

'This is amazing!' crowed Spud. 'You can play any part you want in India, and they go along with it!'

₹

Chapter 7

Special Requests

I hadn't been sure how Spud would fit in with the Indians, but I needn't have worried. Their respect for a fat (read: wealthy), bald (read: holy), and crazy (read: touched by the gods) little Irishman was wonderful to behold. They patted his head for good luck, offered their babies for blessings, and kept asking him to adopt them. The ruder and more direct he became, the more they seemed to like him. They picked up on the fact that Spud didn't give a fig about anything. What they saw was what they got. And in a society where true feelings were often hidden behind a mask of fake politeness, that kind of attitude was a real novelty.

Spud adapted quickly to India. Yes, he could be crass and childish, but he could also be civil, even philosophical, when it suited him. In two short days, despite the unfortunate incident with the Sikh policeman, he proved to be a lively, easygoing travelling companion. He was always fun to be with and always useful to have around. I could tell he had what it would take to jumpstart my small market operation, launching it into a large scale concern. I could hardly wait to get started.

Unfortunately, the first step towards big business was to board an early train to Jaipur. The train was called the Pink

City Express, and it left New Delhi railway station at the unearthly time of 5.50am. Still tired and jet-lagged, I crashed on an available seat and hoped to catch some sleep. But the noise around me rose, and with a degree of horror I realised I was on perhaps the only rail carriage in India filled with thirty-two philosophers.

How did I know this? Well, for one thing, each one of them held a book called *The Knowledge*. They enthusiastically debated conundrums like 'Why is life?' and 'What is God?' Confirmation arrived when Spud yelled out, 'Who's got a degree in philosophy?' and thirty-two hands shot up.

Five hours later we arrived in Jaipur—the picturesque 'pink city' of Rajasthan—and checked into the Megh Niwas hotel in Bani Park, the guesthouse run by my friend, Colonel Fateh Singh. He greeted us warmly when we walked through his hotel's doors, obviously in an expansive mood. The Gulf War was raging, and he was wishing himself in the thick of it. Gesturing enthusiastically, he ushered us outside to meet his ex-army buddies who had been waiting for him on the back lawn, mapping out battle strategies. Later that night the lawn was invaded by tents and tables, and spirited conversations about the Gulf bounced around the VIP party.

At one point a drunken customs official from Delhi airport sidled up and hissed in my ear, 'I can get anything through for you...except *drugs!*' Minutes later he reappeared and confided with even more urgency, 'I can get anything through for you...except *explosives!*'

Around midnight, the Colonel cornered me in my room and offered me an arms contract. 'Frank,' he said, 'you know that fridge I asked you to bring me from UK? Well, now that I have put my thinking cap on, I would prefer you to bring me the nose cone of a Patriot missile. Could you do this thing? It will fit in your hand luggage, I am sure. In fact, bring me any convenient part of western defence system. Anything better than Pakistan!'

Colonel Fateh Singh, retired, ran this small guesthouse in Jaipur with his attractive, unassuming wife, Indu. What I liked most about the Colonel, and the reason I could listen to him for hours on end, was that he was so magnificently larger than life. Every time we met he had a new scheme on the go, a fresh, grand vision of international enterprise. Indu, on the other hand, was easier to please. She delighted in the tea kettle or the shortbread biscuits I brought her from England.

If there was one thing I knew by now, it was that the more enthusiastic Fateh was about his pet projects, the more likely they were to end in failure. The previous summer, for instance, he had taken it into his head to export every Kashmiri carpet from Jaipur to London. Only after they'd been sent did he discover, to his great chagrin, that nobody trusted Kashmiri carpets any more. They only wanted cheap imitations. Unfazed, he changed tack and began buying land in the middle of the Rajasthani desert, planning to plant the biggest rose farm in northern India. To my surprise this scheme worked, but only because Indu, the quietly smiling power behind the throne, had a fondness for English-style rose jam. Long after Fateh's initial enthusiasm had waned, she insisted he go through with it.

I had a soft spot for Indu. Fateh was terminally anglicized, proudly sporting old-school ties and blazers, and sipping at his exclusive collection of old Scotch whiskies. In contrast, Indu was the very model of Indian hospitality. It was because of her that their humble, out-of-town hotel hosted so many foreign patrons. She welcomed each guest with a tray of silver-service tea, served on the lawn by quiet servants in cummerbunds, and introduced them to the resident parrots and peacocks. In the afternoons, she encouraged them to play croquet, and to ease the inexhaustible evening heat by attending impromptu puppet shows on the cool green lawns. To round things off, she guided them inside to watch the English news on television at 10pm, then outside again to visit Fateh's mobile bar. There they dutifully remained until—several cocktails later—they lost consciousness.

Spud and I were planning a trip with the Colonel to pick up more jewellery. But over an English breakfast of boiled eggs and real English tea, Fateh made two new suggestions.

'You should not put all your money into silk and silver,' he said, holding his hands palm-up as if they cradled every penny. 'You should diversify into fashion clothing. This is something Jaipur is famous for.'

Before Spud or I could question the idea, he also suggested that rather than lugging all our Pushkar silk home by hand, we should find a proper freight agent to fly it back for us.

'And I have a solution for both,' he added, grinning. 'We must visit a local handicrafts emporium called Texstyles in Chameliwala Market.'

Texstyles was run by a portly little character named Gordhan Agarwal, and I instantly took to him. Physically, I noted with fascination, Gordhan looked like an overweight hobbit. Small and squat, with no neck at all (just a succession of chins), he was possessed of a large belly, a round moon face, and a vulturine nose which hooked down towards his fat lips. His party trick was to lick his prominent proboscis with the tip of his tongue. The one thing that saved Gordhan from the ridiculous were his eyes, which twinkled with impish humour.

Gordhan did business for fun first and money second. In

India, that made him an original. He was one of those ultra-efficient Indians who could split their brain into five or six separate compartments, each of them performing a complicated task to perfection.

Spud was not so sure of the little man. Sometime later, having pulled Gordhan aside to discuss the export of our silk, he returned to me with a bemused look on his face. 'This silk is not a problem,' he reported, 'as long as Gordhan goes to Delhi and has a talk with the silk inspector. According to Gordhan, the silk inspector will "enjoy" him because Gordhan will "make with the Black Label" and bribe him with whisky.'

It hadn't occurred to me that exporting our silk would be a problem. I'd never even considered that there was a ban on sending it abroad. Gordhan explained, in breathless, near-unintelligible English, that several other countries—notably China—had insisted on the ban in order to protect their own silk exports. There was something called 'baksheesh', a popular form of unofficial bribery, which Gordhan could use to get *around* the ban, but he wasn't promising anything.

Unsure of how to proceed, I decided to take the Colonel's advice. I ordered a load of stuff from Gordhan—mainly patterned waistcoats, velvet purses, and embroidered wall-hangings—to cover our bets. Oddly, just as Spud and I were finalising the deal, Gordhan informed us that, 'velvet purse are going Saddam Hussein.' Even worse, 'wall-hanging not available because of Guleff'. When I asked what the Gulf War had to do with wall-hangings, Gordhan shrugged.

'Pakistan border is seize. All embroidery item come from Pakistan.'

He didn't know who had seized the Pakistan border, but he was pretty sure it was Saddam Hussein.

In the evening, Gordhan treated us, his new foreign friends, to dinner. At the meal we learnt Gordhan was a good, almost extreme, Hindu. He didn't smoke or drink, he didn't eat meat, and he was strictly non-egg. He was also, though he didn't look it, very rich. The threadbare shirt he wore, along with the moth-eaten jumper and beaten-up leather sandals, were part of an act which created the illusion of poverty in an attempt to deter theft. The throwaway remark that he had £100,000 of interest at his local bank rapidly dispelled this myth. Yet he never tired of telling us throughout the meal that he was a 'poor man who makes no profit.'

At the end of the evening an even fatter individual turned up, driving a tiny transit van. This was Gordhan's son, Girish, and he had come to collect both his father and his daily pint of ice cream. The sheer bulk of Girish was awesome. His name meant 'King of the Mountains,' and he certainly lived up to it. Only seventeen years of age, he was already twice the size of his father. He also carried twice the responsibility. Gordhan had given him "Silver Mines", the shop opposite his, and foreign buyers trooped in and out of it all day long, buying jewellery.

'Yeah, I spoke to Girish earlier on,' Spud informed me, 'and while these buyers bitched and complained and generally gave him a hard time, he just sat there like a sleepy Buddha, switching in mood between childish tantrums and stoical resignation. He never gets a holiday, he never takes a day off, his average lunch break is only eight minutes, and he never stops thinking about business. An ideal son for Gordhan really!'

Spud also discovered that all the jewellery we had ordered from the Colonel originated with Girish. This meant Fateh was no longer necessary. From now on we would buy all our silver direct from Girish. Not only was it a cheaper option, but we could also export it—along with our clothes from Gordhan and our Pushkar silk—from one place.

Now all we had to do was buy some silk. 'I heard it down the grapevine,' grumbled a worried Spud as we boarded the bus on to Ajmer, 'that Ivan is trying to buy every piece of silk in Pushkar. We'd better get our skates on or there won't be any left!'

But I wasn't worried. Yes, there were a finite number of second-hand sarees for sale at any one time, but I had already phoned Mendu, my silk supplier in Pushkar, to make sure he had stock. I had even wired Mendu some money to make doubly sure of some stock. So what could possibly go wrong?

Three hours later, having taken the two-rupee 'pilgrim bus' over the Snake Mountain from Ajmer, we arrived at the Pushkar Palace hotel. The hotel was an old favourite of mine. I liked it for its wacky staff, its breezy, palm-fronded terrace, and its amazing sunset views over the holy lake. I also liked that this imposing whitewashed structure, which had originally been built as a royal hunting lodge, had anti-elephant spikes on its huge wooden doors.

The first thing I did on arrival was grab my camera. The first thing Spud did was complain. He had discovered that Pushkar was totally vegetarian, which meant no meat—not even eggs. He was distraught. When Jagat Singh, the hotel manager, was heading out to Ajmer later on, he asked if we wanted anything, Spud shouted, 'Yeah, a pound of sausages!' Jagat was not amused.

I was glad to be back in Pushkar. It was a magical place, my second 'home' in the world, and I knew I would return time and again. I well remembered my first impressions of the place: a small jewel in the navel of India, ablaze with its colourful mix of pilgrims, hippies, merchants, and holy men,

39

its outdoor menagerie of cows, pigs, dogs, and monkeys. Most of all I remembered being lulled by its unique blend of romantic mysticism and hard-nosed business practice.

When I had first arrived in 1985, just as the tourists had begun to trickle in, I had found it wonderfully unspoilt. The ancient buildings were whitewashed and flaky, the lake was peaceful (apart from a few leaping carp), and the sleepy marketplace was dotted with a few browsing backpackers.

But the old Pushkar was changing fast. In the short space of six months, it had morphed from a quiet, laidback hippy outpost into a busy, bustling hive of business activity. Hordes of foreign buyers were now in town, and the long, winding market street around the lake and bathing *ghats* was full of newly built hotels, cafés, and restaurants. Everyone was there for the same thing: second-hand sarees. Wherever we looked, Spud and I saw lorryloads of silk, freshly arrived from Bombay and Ahmedabad, manned by rag merchants who had paid a fraction of their original worth—say 30 pence for a £50 saree—to bored housewives wanting to clear out their bottom drawers.

'What a *buzz!*' enthused Spud. 'You can almost smell the money!'

A gauntlet of hallooing traders and shopkeepers lined the market street, all vying for our attention and our dollars. Beggars and so-called holy men rose from the pavement to block our way, and *puja* boys—the kids who sold prayers for money at the ghats—kept stuffing rose petals in our hands, trying to lure us down to the lake.

We fell into Mendu's shop with a sigh of relief. 'Is Ivan here yet?' I asked, trying to sound unconcerned, but Mendu shook his head.

'Not come. Today *lucky* day, *big* stock!'

I shot Spud a look of triumph, and the two of us dug in, choosing the best pieces. Four hours later, I turned to Spud.

'Well, that's *that* done, then,' I said with a smirk. 'Four thousand pieces of top-of-the-range silk with a street value of £40,000. Eat your heart out, Ivan!'

But Spud wasn't listening. He was staring outside, distracted by a manic little figure dancing up and down in the street.

'Who's that?' he asked.

'Oh, that's Lalit Jain. Mister Bullshit.'

'Mister *who?*'

'Mister Bullshit. That's the name I gave him a couple of years back, when we first met. He stopped me in the street and said, "Come my shop! It is cool like supercomputer and we can talk bullshit for the laughing!" So, he's been Mister Bullshit ever since.'

'Why do you talk to him?' marvelled Spud. 'He's a wanker!'

'He's also the biggest moneychanger in town,' I explained. 'There's a huge black market for foreign currency in India, and he can give us up to fifteen per cent more for our dollars than any bank. It pays to keep on the right side of him.'

Once we were on the street, Lalit stuck out his hand and proclaimed himself 'double-delighted' to see me again. 'Ah, Mister Frank,' he declared. 'Famous writer! You are always on my dreams!'

Spud stared at him, agog. 'Well, you're certainly on *something*,' he remarked.

Which was true, since Lalit had something of a drinking problem. We encountered him later on, weaving unevenly down the road on a moped. 'I am having double-much fun!' he giggled happily.

Then he ran into a sacred cow.

₹

Chapter 8

The Ups and Downs of Spud

The following day, Spud – putting aside his earlier reservations – had occasion to use Mister Bullshit. He had heard Ivan was coming into town and, not being content with having bought up all the best silk, he decided to rub Ivan's nose in it. Somehow he persuaded Lalit to loan him every black market rupee in town for a few hours, then he took over the shop opposite Mendu's, setting himself up as a moneychanger.

'Hallo, Mister Moscow!' he shouted as Ivan came into sight. He did a frighteningly good impersonation of the local dialect. 'Change dollar? Good rate for yoooou!'

If Ivan was startled at the sight of Spud sitting up there, surrounded by piles of Indian banknotes, he didn't show it. He kept his cool. He went into a quick huddle with his brother, Viktor, then narrowed his eyes and asked, 'What rate you geeve?'

Spud gave him a sly, conspiratorial grin and whispered, 'Twenty per cent better than bank. Only for *you!*'

Viktor tugged Ivan away. 'We know this guy. He's crazy! Let's check somewhere else!'

But when they did, they discovered nobody else had any

black market money for sale. Minutes later, they were back at Spud's 'shop', thrusting all their foreign currency at him.

Spud wasn't through with them. 'So sorry,' he said triumphantly. 'You had your chance. Now you're fucked!'

Mendu, and every other Indian within earshot, laughed Ivan out of town.

Unfortunately, Ivan had the last laugh. Three weeks later, back in England, we waited with bated breath as our first consignment from Gordhan was unloaded outside Spud's house. There were nine large boxes in all, but something was missing. Perplexed, we dug into the boxes, checking our inventory. Waistcoats, wall-hangings, bedspreads, and purses all flew over Spud's shoulder. Then he turned to me.

'Where is our *silk?*'

It was a good question, and one to which only Gordhan had the answer. Over the phone Gordhan explained he had tried to export the silk along with the other goods, but had failed. 'No get licence for silk export,' he'd moaned to Spud. 'Better you send gift parcel!'

Spud asked how this worked, and Gordhan suggested sending the silk as forty separate 'gift' parcels in order to circumvent Indian customs and avoid heavy export duties. The important thing, he had stressed, was to send each ten-kilo parcel to a different address in the UK. This was to disguise the fact that they contained commercial goods and not gifts.

But Spud had been impatient. Without telling me, he instructed Gordhan to put his address on every single parcel. As a result, they all got confiscated by English customs.

And from being rupee millionaires one day, we were broke the next.

For the first time in our partnership, I was furious with Spud. 'If you didn't have forty friends or family to send those parcels to, why didn't you say so?'

His grin never wavered. 'I don't do sorries,' he said.

I considered cutting my maverick 'friend' loose and going solo again, then thought better of it. A little voice deep inside told me we still had a future together. And this little voice overpowered the *other* little voice, which nagged constantly.

'Frank,' it urged, 'you're losing your Buddhist centre. You're on a dangerous roller-coaster, and if you have any sense you'll get off right now.'

Just as I was about to get off, just as I was ready to throw in the towel, I received a phone call from Gordhan. My portly Indian friend had been back to Delhi airport, servicing another customer, where he had discovered twelve of Spud's forty parcels sitting in a backroom store. Gordhan had tipped a customs guy £100 to release them and was now posting them to London. He gave each one a different address to ensure their safe arrival.

I couldn't believe my luck. If Gordhan had been standing in front of me, I would have kissed him.

A few days later, with all twelve parcels in hand, we were back in business—albeit on a much smaller scale than anticipated.

'We've got to move this stuff quickly,' Spud informed me, 'so we can buy back all the silk we lost. And that means more market stalls.'

The very next day Spud redeemed himself in my eyes by barging his way into north London's biggest market, Camden, and obtaining a permanent double-pitch there. His sister had 'connections', he said. Besides, the market manager was shit-scared of him. Lighting a huge gob of Pushkar temple *dhoop* (incense) beneath the manager's office and smoking him out of the building had terrified the poor guy.

Camden was the ideal venue for selling silk. It was more 'alternative' than St Martin's, drew a bigger crowd, and commanded better prices. In a matter of weeks Spud and I were solvent again, and planning our next move.

On 11th March 1991 we worked our first festival. It wasn't much, just a one day music event at Hythe, near Folkestone. We arrived early, around 7am, and seized the best pitch, right up by the performance stage.

'This is where we want to be,' Spud said, smirking. He grabbed a "Psychic Tent" and tossed it into the field below. 'I bet they didn't "see" that coming!'

Business was slow until dusk, mainly due to the rain, then it became hectic. The night was so dark people couldn't see what they were buying, but by then they were too drunk or stoned to care.

'What colour's this bag?' they asked.

'It's black,' we said. Suits you, sir!'

'What stone's in that ring?' they asked.

'Black star sapphire,' we said. 'How lucky can you get?'

If they didn't have money, they paid in other ways. 'I got some wicked mushrooms, man,' offered one punter. 'I want that floppy hat!'

'I'm just off the boat from the Dam,' suggested another. 'Here's an ounce of primo black for that pair of tie-dye dungarees!'

If they didn't have drugs, they brought over a burger or a few beers. At the end of the night, we were so stoned and drunk we could barely stand up, let alone pack away. None of the other vendors made much at this event. Spud and I went home with over a grand.

The Hythe gig was significant in one other respect. It marked the first step on the road to Spud's planned wholesale empire. At the end of the fair we came away with a list of ten shops to whom we could sell, and finally saw an end to working six days a week on a market stall.

Only one thing stuck in Spud's craw. It was the Petrovs again, and this time they meant business. Ivan and Viktor had just returned from Delhi with eight suitcases apiece of saree clothing, and they were flooding all the London markets with it. To make things worse, they were being regularly restocked by a dozen young hippies. The Petrovs apparently paid the kids to go to Pushkar and bring back forty kilos of silk every month.

'What a brilliant fucking idea!' spat Spud. 'Why didn't *we* think of it?'

The summer over, we returned to Pushkar – only to find a full-scale 'saree war' in progress. Truckloads of sarees bound for one shop were being diverted (bribed) on their way from Bombay to go to other shops, and the central marketplace now resembled a bull run on the stock market, with traders and silk merchants hysterically exchanging money and orders. One wholesaler stole his 'friend's' glasses, forcing him to buy a load of damaged stock 'unseen'. Another spiked a competitor's coffee with acid, taking him out of the game completely.

Spud waited for an opportunity to sabotage Ivan. Then he took it. We were sitting in a café, enjoying a banana *lassi*, when a distressed—and very voluptuous—Italian tourist chanced by. Her pouting bottom lip quivered enticingly, and her sash-bound breasts followed suit.

'I lose my passport!' she wailed to the street. 'I cannot go home!'

'Oh dear,' commiserated Spud in a rare display of pity. 'Can I be of help?'

The sultry siren ceased trembling and sat at our table. 'How can you help?'

'Well, I saw you in the market earlier. You were talking to that Russian guy, Ivan.'

'Yes. So what of it?'

'He's a good-looking geezer, isn't he? Do you like him?'

'Yes, I like him.'

Spud leaned across the table towards her. 'How much do you like him?

She flushed. 'He is very nice.'

'Okay, well,' he said, leaning back in his chair, 'I'm going to give you three hundred English pounds. I want you to be extra-special 'nice' to him for a few days. Keep him in his room. Don't let him out for any reason.'

She gasped, scandalised. 'You think I am *prostitute?*'

'Nah, as I said, I'm just trying to help.' Spud's smug grin was back. 'You want the money or not?'

She took the money.

It was six long days before Ivan emerged from his hotel room. Then, just as he prepared to settle down and do business again, he stuck his hand in his secret money stash, only to find someone had put a cobra in it. Apparently the Italian temptress had warmed to her mission and gone the extra mile.

Poor Ivan. Once bitten, twice shy; he left town in a coma. Though not, we soon found out, before his brother Viktor had bought up every piece of silk in town, damaged or not. That crafty move put the rest of us out of business.

Spud was enraged. 'Right. That's it!' he spat. 'Victor's going to the top of my death list. With Ivan a close number two.'

'You've got a *death* list?'

'Yeah,' he said, crossing his arms over his chest. 'Me and

my mate cooked it up in the army.'

'You've got a *mate?*' I exclaimed. 'Where's he, then?'

'What, fat Pete? He's in Parkhurst for molesting a bus driver.'

'Was the bus driver on your death list?'

Spud waved a hand, dismissing the idea. 'No, Pete did him for free. A bit like I'm going to do Mendu right now, given half the chance!'

Spud located Mendu playing cricket out back, and demanded to know where our vanload of silk was. Mendu shrugged and said, 'Gone Pakistan.'

Spud promptly broke his bat in half.

'Better you take T-shirt!' offered Mendu, still unaware of the danger he was in. 'T-shirt good!'

This suggestion did not go down well with Spud. Now that his Harry Enfield 'loads a money' dream was in tatters, he informed Mendu that T-shirt was *not* good. He wanted silk and nothing but.

'No buying T-shirt?' wheedled Mendu. 'For you, T-shirt *better!*'

Spud lost it. 'I don't want T-shirt!' he exploded. 'Don't say T-shirt again, or I'll pull out all your teeth!'

Mendu's jaw dropped. 'No angry!' he bleated, then he ran out of the shop.

I found myself curiously amused. Up until now, everyone in Pushkar had thought Spud a 'very nice man.' This was strange, because I was well aware Spud was wont to kick down doors and threaten loss of limbs when things didn't go his way. Only the previous day, he had told one supplier, 'I'm going to kill all your cattle.'

The supplier had smiled nervously, then stuttered, 'Ha, ha, ha! You are a good joking man!'

That was moments before Spud punched his cow.

It was the same with the name-calling. Spud had endured being called *takala*, or baldy, up to now. Today, when the abuse extended to 'Full Moon!' or 'Sethi Ganga!' (a bald film star), he found a way of avenging himself. For every Indian who shouted *'Ganju!'* (egghead) at him, he shouted 'gan-DU! or 'gay-boy!' back at them, followed by various threats of horrible injuries.

Unfortunately, the Indians weren't the only ones who suffered Spud's spite. With his dream of silk gone forever, Spud started laying into fellow travellers.

'What a bunch of losers!' he sniffed. 'Lots of manic traders charging up and down the market with no time for chit-chat, only interested in filling their orders. And then there's the wobbly-heads sitting around in lakeside cafés, playing guitars, and getting wrecked on *bhang lassis!*'

Intrigued, I asked Spud what he meant by wobbly-heads.

'Oh, that's easy,' he retorted. 'A wobbly-head is someone who's been in India for two months and looks like they've been here for five years. They've got off the plane, put on their hippy glad-rags, and charged off to Goa or some place they can live for next to nothing. Then they spend half their day smoking their chillums and the other half conversing in broken Hindi with local holy men.'

To make his day complete, Spud was next accosted by Lalit Jain, alias Mister Bullshit.

'Hello you!' brayed Lalit, apparently unaware of the shift in climate. 'You are my underwear friend!'

Spud told him to get lost, but Lalit pressed on. 'I couldn't sleep last night because you are not here!'

Spud eyed him warily and suggested he lay off the *bhang*.

Undeterred, Lalit laid his palms on Spud's bald pate—not

generally a good idea at the best of times—and asked, 'What are you growing in your head?'

Spud leaned over and whispered something in his ear.

Lalit ran off screaming.

On our last day in Pushkar, Spud was still in a foul mood. He strode into the market and promptly took over someone's shop. To be fair, before he actually stepped in, he took a few minutes to observe a rookie shopkeeper who had no idea of how to sell to tourists. Then he walked behind the table, shoved the man behind him, and informed him, 'You're crap, mate. Move over and watch me.'

Over the next hour, much to the amusement of surrounding Indians, Spud sold two expensive wall-hangings, did three big money-changing deals, and offloaded a horrible brass statue that had been collecting dust for years. The shopkeeper was so impressed he offered Spud a job.

I was not so impressed. As far as I could see, Spud was spinning out of control. Everything had been okay when I was in charge of the buying end of things and Spud was in charge of the selling, but now that the roles were reversing I was fast losing track. How come, for instance, we had run out of money? All of it had apparently gone on silver and handicrafts. We even owed thousands of pounds to people like Gordhan.

'I don't understand this,' I told Spud as we retraced our steps back to England. 'The bigger we get, the more we seem to owe.'

'Don't worry about it,' Spud assured me with a familiar grin. 'We've got lots of stock now, haven't we? And remember: stock is *power!*'

₹

Chapter 9

What Makes a Rupee Millionaire?

Time proved Spud right. After a good Christmas and an even better show in Torquay, where we collected a load of new shops to wholesale to, we finally moved into profit. Not that I saw much of it. Spud held a tight grip on the purse strings and allowed us both just £2,000 a month, barely enough to pay our rent and necessary expenses. The rest went back, naturally, into more stock.

'What's the plan now?' I asked Spud. 'Why can't we just rest up for a bit and enjoy the fruits of our labours?'

He looked disgusted at the question. 'Because we're in for the long haul, mate! And that means working our bollocks off until we've made twenty grand!'

When I enquired why twenty grand specifically, Spud asked, 'You want to be a rupee millionaire, don't you? Well, that's twenty grand. The first twenty grand is the hardest. After that, money makes money. It's simple mathematics. The more you have, the more you can invest, the more profit you make. And we don't stop there. We go on from being rupee millionaires to being Belgian Franc millionaires, then German Deutschmark millionaires. Then, after we've worked our way through all the Western currencies, we'll end up being actual millionaires!'

I stared. 'You mean in sterling?'

'Yeah! Fuck, why not? And when you're an actual millionaire, you won't be whining and complaining that I worked you so hard. You'll be grateful. You'll be the *man!*'

Even with this kind of promise, I wasn't so sure. I hadn't had a day off in months and was close to collapse.

'What's the big rush?' I asked. 'Now we've actually got some money, why aren't we getting drunk and celebrating?'

Spud's face split with an evil grin. 'Because I've just had a word with Liberty's, that big department store in Regent Street, that's why. They want us to snap up every piece of old embroidery in Rajasthan. According to their head buyer, it's running out real fast, so we've got to get our skates on.'

'Okayyy,' I said slowly, 'but we're not going to make much out of heavy bedspreads and wall-hangings. They cost more to send home than to buy them.'

'You're missing the point,' replied Spud. 'If we get in with Liberty's, the largest chain of Asian textile shops in the country, we'll be made for life. Let Ivan have his little silk empire. We'll be dealing with the big boys!'

*

In February 1992 we touched down once more in Delhi airport. This time, however, we had forty grand to spend. Half of it would be going on jewellery for our markets. The other half was slotted for old embroidery for Liberty's.

Within minutes of arrival, Spud caused a near-riot. 'Check this out!' he said, stuffing a wrapped handkerchief into my hands.

The package wriggled. 'What is it?' I asked.

His expression reminded me of a little boy with a freshly caught frog. 'It's a two and a half inch cockroach!' he crowed happily. 'I found it perched on the urinal in the immigration hall. Don't you want to see it?'

'No!' I cried, dropping the offending hankie. 'No, I don't!'

Six neat lines of passengers queued up with their passports instantly broke rank as the busy beetle scurried over their luggage and ran up skirts and trouser legs.

'Oh my *God!*' shrieked a flight attendant. 'It's in my *hair!*'

Her friend screamed, then shouted, 'Why doesn't someone do something?'

Spud, ever the considerate traveller, decided to do something. He seized a long broom from a passing cleaner and beat Ms Hysterical round the head with it.

'I think he got it!' cried an old lady standing beside me.

But no, he hadn't. He had simply knocked over the flight attendant. The panicked insect, having been dislodged from its high-rise perch, promptly scuttled off in search of a new haven. It took Spud, still wielding the broom, five more minutes to chase it round the concourse and stomp it into oblivion.

'Ooh, what a brave young man you are!' the old lady congratulated him. 'Someone should give you a medal!'

We stepped out of the airport and straight into a waiting taxi. 'Let's get out of here,' muttered Spud, glancing over his shoulder. 'Before they find out who put that roach there in the first place!'

Over the next few hours, while Spud dozed in the back seat, I found myself wondering why he was dragging us back to India so soon, and on such a weird mission. I had to suspect an ulterior motive. I'd been in his train wreck of a house a couple of weeks earlier and had seen the clothes and debris strewn all around since Lou had left him. His computer had been open, and I noticed he'd applied to several online dating agencies. Not surprisingly, his grim, unsmiling face had elicited zero replies. Nor had his "chat up" line, which said simply, 'My name's Spud. I'm coming into money. Do you fancy a shag?'

He was lonely. I could see that. He was working his butt off—and mine, too—in the hope that a million rupees might sort out his sex life. I prayed to Buddha he would be successful. If he didn't get some action soon, I doubted I would, either.

In Jaipur, we tried to check in at the Colonel's guesthouse, but it proved impossible. Some kind of wedding party was going on out back of his hotel, and a huge pavilion had been erected—dangerously close to the edge of his new swimming pool. Inebriated guests wove in and out of its canvas walls.

'It's one of Fateh's latest pet projects,' confided Indu with a frown. 'I just hope none of these fellows drowns!'

As I watched, Fateh drifted over to one of his ex-army buddies, a strict Hindu, and began scoffing at the sacred nature of cows. 'There is nothing in Hinduism which says cows should be allowed in the middle of the road,' he stated. 'Neither can I find anything in the *Gita* which says we can't eat cow meat. I've eaten tons of the stuff!'

Before his guest could respond to this blasphemous piece of news, Fateh launched into an even more contentious story.

'During the war with Pakistan,' he recalled fondly, 'we laid an extensive minefield. We got the citizens of the town to leave, but they left their cattle behind. In time, a cow wandered into the minefield. All my soldiers were in a panic, so I suggested, 'Why don't we shoot it?' They stared at me with horror in their eyes. 'What? Shoot a cow? Just before a war is about to start? Ayeee! What bad luck!' But none of us could sleep. The cow kept moaning right through the night. The next morning, I got my gun and shot it. Funnily enough, the men respected me for that.'

Fateh's elderly guest tottered away, shaking his head in rage. A small, almost imperceptible smile played across my friend's lips. If I hadn't known better, I'd say he'd just made that story up.

Fortified by the Colonel's drinks trolley, we took rooms at the Arya Niwas, just off M.I. Road. This was another of my favourite hotels – a clean and cosy oasis of calm, with a wide green lawn to relax in and the best budget food in town.

The following evening, after checking some silver from Girish, I took Spud to the cinema. This wasn't just any old cinema, but the Raj Mandir, one of the biggest flick-houses in Asia. The vast lobby screamed with art-deco, and within the theatre lights flashed urgently around the screen whenever a film reached a crescendo. We were there to see *Hum*, the biggest blockbuster of 1992. It starred Amitabh Bacchan, India's answer to Rambo. And like all Bollywood films, it totally defied description.

'What did you think of that?' I asked Spud afterwards.

He blinked at me, confused. 'It's like a cross between *On The Waterfront* and *Saturday Night Fever,* innit? The heroine spent most of the film either being doused with water or chased around a disco floor by maniac gangsters wielding bicycle pumps!'

Leaving the cinema by rickshaw, we came across the ultimate 'veggie' of Jaipur. He was even more extreme than Gordhan. The driver of the rickshaw, a Mr Kumar, was not only non-meat and non-egg, but non-onion as well.

Spud shook his head, mystified. 'I can understand about not eating cows and pigs. Even eggs. But how can anybody be offended at the death of an onion?'

After we'd sorted out our silver and left half our cash with Gordhan, we proceeded to Pushkar in search of old embroidery. But, as I had secretly suspected, there was none left. All those stunning, turn-of-the century *zari* bedspreads, shiny with gold and silver threadwork, had been sold. All that was left was a dusty collection of salmon-pink pieces produced around the time of the 1947 partition. Even these had doubled in price since our last visit.

'Well, that's that, then!' Spud muttered grimly. 'We're fucked.'

'Not necessarily,' I mused. 'What about Jaiselmer?'

'What *about* Jaiselmer?'

'I was there a few years ago, and the whole place was simply dripping with old embroidery: wall-hangings, bedspreads, cushion covers, the lot. The city has fallen on hard times lately, and I've heard the people are being forced to sell off all their antique handicrafts. As far as I'm aware, they're still doing it.'

Spud's eyes widened. 'Why didn't you say so before?' he asked. 'When's the next bus?'

The bus ride to Jodhpur took a long six hours, after which we had to book a ten-hour overnight train on to Jaiselmer. This was easier said than done. The Jodhpur railway booking office was famously inefficient.

'It only opens at 4pm,' I informed an impatient Spud, 'except when it doesn't. And it won't open for a whole host of reasons, like festivals, holidays, sick relatives, or if the booking clerk has an extended tea break. Why do you think Liberty's didn't go to Jaiselmer themselves? It's a total nightmare to get there!'

The booking office didn't open until 5.30pm, and when it

did the clerk smiled placidly and informed us, 'So sorry, bedroll not available.'

The non-availability of a bedroll was a serious matter. Without one we were looking at ten hours of insomnia, lying on a couple of bare planks in a cramped bunk bed. When the clerk indicated that a bedroll might be available if some money was forthcoming, I promptly laid fifty rupees on him. He returned ten minutes later carrying two brand new bedrolls which he had just nicked off a train headed to Delhi.

At two the next morning a loud banging on the door of our compartment woke us up.

'You can't come in,' I mumbled. 'Go away!'

'Open door! This is the guard!' came a shout from the corridor.

'Go *away*,' repeated Spud, fumbling in the dark. 'I can't open the door!'

'Why not? Why you cannot open door?' The voice had developed a definite edge.

Spud sighed. 'Because the fucking light's gone out, and I can't see where the lock is.'

'Why you not open?' the guard demanded. 'If you can close, you can open!'

I could sense Spud's rising irritation and hoped the guard would just go away. Quickly.

'Well, the light was on then, wasn't it?' he said. 'Now I can't find the damn thing.'

There was a pause, then the voice shouted, *'Hello bedroll!'*

With a grunt, Spud finally got the door open. A troll-like figure with a woolly sock on its head stepped into the compartment. *'I am HERE!'* it announced.

As one we asked the man why he was here.

'Jaiselmer coming,' he replied, holding out his hands.

'Deposit me bedroll!'

With a growl, Spud stepped toward him and he took one step back, giving us the opportunity to slam the door on him. Problem resolved, we settled back onto our bedrolls for another three hours sleep.

₹

Chapter 10

Mister Bank-Rupert

It was 5.30am when we finally pulled into Jaiselmer. Poking our heads out the train window, we caught a brief glimpse of the city's majestic 12th century fort rising from the flat desert floor. Then a cloud of sooty steam from the nearby engine forced us, coughing violently, back into the compartment again. I made a mental note to sit at the back of the train the next time.

Outside the station I braced myself for the usual crowd of jeep drivers wanting to take me to their choice of hotel and collect their commission. Brushing them all aside, I led Spud to the jeep driving to *my* choice of hotel: the Paradise, situated at the top of the old fort.

I liked the Paradise for three reasons: it had the quietest rooms in town, there were hardly any rabid dogs around, and all the shops were close by. Chandra, the smiley owner, gave me his best room, right on the fort ramparts, overlooking the desert. After we'd settled he directed us to the new Trio restaurant, just inside the fort walls, for a 'happy breakfast.' Trio, we found, was Jaiselmer's only claim to a decent restaurant in the western sense. It had a proper table service, turbaned and cummerbunded waiters, and a tastefully embroidered menu, at the bottom of which they'd printed, 'Thank you for patronising us.'

Spud ordered the Murgh Biriani, which translated as 'Less of chicken with egg,' while I had 'Cream of Chicken Soup – the Soup which is known to You and Everyone.'

Pleasantly full, we headed out to start shopping. It was far easier than we'd imagined—all the embroidery we were looking for was located in one shop called Damoder Handicrafts, situated just down from our hotel at the fourth fort gate.

Damoder, the proprietor, was a young, roly-poly guy with a pencil-thin moustache and an oily grin. He was very glad to see us. He was very glad to see us because he had just bought up all the old zari bedspreads in town and couldn't find anyone to buy them. Plus he owed an impressive £20,000 to his various suppliers.

The shop was stacked to the ceiling with the most beautiful pieces we had ever seen.

'Bugger me!' Spud muttered respectfully. 'Liberty's will just eat this stuff up!'

With some effort, Damoder climbed slowly to his feet. 'Buy lot!' he wheedled. 'I am poor man. I sell you cheap. I am bank-rupert!'

Apparently the only things that could save him from bank-rupertcy were our dollars. And since the price was right, we quickly emptied our pockets and transported the entire contents of Damoder's shop into a waiting jeep. Two hours later, after a short rest, we were on our way back to Pushkar, mission accomplished.

Or so we thought.

Ten minutes out of Jaiselmer the jeep blew a tyre, and all our goods were tipped into the road.

'Fair enough,' I said. 'I wanted to do a bit of sightseeing anyway!'

Spud shook his head in disbelief and hailed a passing camel.

Back at the Paradise, I tried to interest Spud in some of the local attractions. Where would he like to go first? The Dop Khana cannon point? The fanciful Salim Singh haveli? The massive Mandir Palace? Or the five ornate merchants' houses collectively known as Patwon Ki Haveli?

Spud just eyed me stonily. 'What's nearest?'

What was nearest were the famous *Jain* temples, just a short walk from the Paradise. I was just stepping up to the entrance when voices were raised behind me.

'Shoe off!' shouted the priest, nearly ripping Spud's flip-flops off his feet.

'Who the fuck are *you?*' cried Spud. He grasped desperately at the ground, vainly trying to recover his footwear.

The irate Jain kicked Spud's shoes down the temple stairs. 'I am priest of this temple! You will respect this place of worship!'

Spud practically vibrated with fury. 'Look here, you holy git!' he ranted. 'If you don't pick those up, we're not going to get along at *all!*'

Both of them were spoiling for a punch-up, so I decided to intervene. Steering Spud away from the angry sage, I guided him inside the temple.

His first sneering words were, 'Is this *it*, then? All we've got here are three hundred cross-eyed, naked fat men!' I suggested he lower his voice, since he was publicly insulting the Jain saints, but Spud was on a roll. 'What are all these polished little fat blokes doing staring at me?' he scoffed.

'They all look the same, they do!'

I decided Spud had had enough sightseeing and ushered him outside, then towards Jaiselmer's famous *bhang* shop.

'What's *bhang,* then?' he demanded.

'It's a stewed juice made from the mashed leaves of the marijuana plant,' I explained, 'and when you put it in a cake or a lassi drink, it can be lethal. Nearly every Indian in Rajasthan smokes, eats, or drinks bhang. It's sacred to Shiva. Though I've only come across four places in all India where it's cool for foreigners to smoke it: Goa, Manali, Pushkar and right here in Jaiselmer. And even then only in the privacy of their own rooms. Anywhere else and they run the risk of a big fine or a lengthy jail sentence.'

We stepped inside the shop, and Spud's curious eyes were everywhere. 'Look at the menu!' he marvelled. 'It tells you exactly what to expect from your experience. "Do not anticipate or analyse," it says. "Just enjoy. You will not sell, drink elephants, jump off all buildings, or turn into an orange, and you will remember most of your experience in the morning".'

'What it does not tell you,' I remarked drily, 'is how to get back to your hotel at night when you're off your head and there's a power-cut.'

I bought four cookies off the guy and later found out that Spud had bought four also. Never mind the elephants. We had a very hard time getting home that night. And we didn't want to remember our experience next morning. We surfaced around noon, with sore eyes and sore heads. Spud had lost a shoe somewhere, and I had no idea where I'd left my hat. We had breakfast when everyone else was taking lunch, then popped in on Mr Bank-Rupert to say our goodbyes since we had little energy to do anything else.

To our great surprise, we found Damoder lounging fatly on his divan, his previously empty shop crammed to the ceiling with yet more spectacular goods.

'Today lucky day!' he cried with glee, struggling to his feet. 'Bedspread go, *toran* come!' Yes, he had spent all our money on highly decorative wall-hangings and was once again bank-rupert.

Spud and I exchanged a look of despair then said in unison, 'Do you take credit cards?'

The trip back to Pushkar should have taken nine hours, but it took twelve because of the minefield of dead animals littering the highway. 'You won't believe this,' Spud woke me to say, 'but I've seen two dead donkeys, a pitted skeleton of a cow, three dead dogs, and a dead lorry driver. I've also noticed a breed of desert goat which appears to be crossed with a lemming. It lingers at the side of the road and deliberately throws itself in front of vehicles which are travelling at eighty miles an hour.'

Spud spent forty minutes in Pushkar, just long enough for a wash and a meal. Then he was off with our truckload of precious embroidery, headed to see Gordhan in Jaipur and to ship everything home. I waved him off with a sigh. For the next week or so, I would be stuck here in Pushkar on my own.

Or so I thought.

I climbed the stairs at the Palace hotel, only to find that my favourite room had been given to someone else. The "someone else" was an old friend of mine, American George, and the room in question was 111, which was the only room in Pushkar with a decent shower and no cockroaches.

I bumped into George on my way to room 112, which cost twice as much for no hot water and a roach in the sink.

'Hey, my man!' brayed George. 'I had no idea you were

comin' into town!'

He slapped my back so hard I nearly dropped my luggage. I stared at George, slack-jawed. In addition to his usual frizzy mop of black hair and round Lennon spectacles, he now sported a long, droopy moustache and a perky little army cap. I couldn't decide who he looked like more: Frank Zappa or "Radar" out of *M*A*S*H**.

George was from Pittsburgh, and he was very intense. He liked loud thrash music, deconstructed jazz, and composing his own songs, which he strummed on a tiny ukulele he'd picked up in a Varanasi backstreet. Grumpy by day and only sociable after dark, George was a real night-bird. He wrote most of his songs in the wee, wee hours, and was fond of dragging people to his room in the evenings and entertaining them with whisky, dope, and endless tunes on his mini-guitar. When he was in a particularly good mood, he waxed lyrical about God, the universe, and (being half-Greek) Greek Orthodox religion.

'Do you believe in God?' I once asked.

'*Totally*, man!' replied George.

I had struck up a friendship with George the previous year when I had rescued the irascible American from a punch-up with an Israeli in Delhi's Paharganj market. He had been strolling past the hippy-dippy Khosla Café on his very first day in India and stopped to investigate.

'Hey man, my name's George!' he had accosted the Israeli sitting there. 'What's yours?'

But the Israeli hadn't responded, just kept staring out at the road.

George couldn't believe his rudeness and growled, 'What's your *problem*, man?' in his ear.

Whereupon the Israeli looked up very slowly and said, 'Do not bother me. I am sitting here. I see dee cow, I see dee holy maaaan, I see dee paan-wallaaah, den I see you. You are not part of my Indian Experience. Go away!'

I stepped in just in time to stop George from committing murder.

The Pushkar shopkeepers liked George. He thought it was because he was so friendly and outgoing. I thought it was because he bought a lot of rubbish they couldn't sell to anyone else. They called him George Bush, partly because he was a Yank, and partly because of his bushy moustache. Every time he walked down the street, it resounded with calls of 'Booosh! Booosh!' and the traders rubbed their hands together in anticipation of approaching dollars.

George's main business was silk. He was back in Pushkar to quadruple his order, and he could not believe I was not buying any silk at all.

'It was good while it lasted,' I explained. 'But ever since Ivan flooded London with damaged silk this summer—the result of his cobra accident—none of our shops will touch the stuff.'

'Where is Ivan?' George asked. 'This is the first time I've hit Pushkar when that mother hasn't hoovered up every piece of silk in town.'

I was surprised he hadn't been informed of the latest news. 'Haven't you heard? He's been in jail for the past four months. He had an argument with his landlord in London, and "someone" decided to settle that argument by blowing up the landlord's house.'

'Someone?'

'Yeah, the courts ruled against Ivan, but I actually don't think it was him.' I hesitated, then said, 'I think it was Spud.'

'Are you serious?'

I shrugged. 'I wouldn't put it past him. He's had Ivan on

66

some kind of "death list" for messing with our business. Plus he's good at blowing up things. He used to work for British Gas.'

'Phew,' George muttered respectfully. 'You English guys sure play rough!'

₹

Chapter 11

Colourful Characters

George was sharing room 111 with an equally crazy American named Amy. She wasn't his girlfriend, but the best friend of his girlfriend, and she had been sent out to be George's 'minder.' As far as I could make out, Amy was supposed to stop him from being picked up by itinerant hippy bimbos.

Amy didn't look like an American. With her olive skin, long raven hair, and aquiline nose I immediately put her down as a continental. One of her parents, I later learnt, was Italian, so I wasn't far wrong. Amy was beautiful but short on conversation. The only thing she waxed lyrical about was the Grateful Dead, her favourite rock band.

How I ended up in bed with her, I'll never know. Perhaps it was the gallons of duty-free scotch and ouzo we put away. I vaguely remember playing a card game of Amy's invention called 'Spit' on the hotel lawn at 2am, but little else. I don't know what happened to George. I think he might have collapsed somewhere with alcohol poisoning.

The next morning passed in a blur. Off in the distance I heard a Grateful Dead tape playing. I think that was Amy in the toilet. My head felt like Hangover Square and I wanted to die.

Was Spud in town, I wondered dimly. Had he pulled the same stroke on me as he had with Ivan, and bribed someone to seduce me? To be honest, I just didn't care.

Breakfast happened at noon. I quickly discovered that George and Amy had a language all of their own. I think it was called American. These two were into 'too much fun' and their stock phrases included 'Thank *you*, motherfucker!' and 'Right *back* at you, girlfriend!' Apart from the Grateful Dead, they had a fixation on *bhang* lassis. These they described as 'truly awesome.' According to them, George and Amy were in India to do some 'serious styling.' George was 'into' shopping and Amy was 'into' vegetarian food. They were like two hyped-up alien hippies, and in my present condition I couldn't understand one word they were saying.

I was just about to retire back to bed when George leapt to his feet and dragged me off to the barber for a 'male bonding' experience. This involved my losing my beard and George his Zappa moustache. George then treated himself to a 'famous head massage', which turned out to be a mistake. The barber whipped out what appeared to be an electric dildo and buffeted George around the cheeks with it until they were red-raw.

Amy didn't like my naked face. I guessed that when she booked herself on a video bus out of Pushkar barely ten minutes after seeing it. Where was she going? To help out some women's development programme in a remote village north of Bikaner.

Yes, that's how bad I looked without a beard.

Strolling into town later on, I was puzzled by the catcalls of 'Two-Up Kusy!' from passing shopkeepers and puja boys. It was only then that I remembered the *second* girl, whom George had picked up two nights before, and who had passed out in my room on the back sofa. She had fled town even earlier than Amy, hoping to hide her embarrassment. Nothing had happened with her of course, but nobody was to know that, so I let the rumour stick. It upped my street-cred no end.

Two days later, Amy returned from her desert sojourn, totally disillusioned with the development programme. The village where she'd stayed was apparently bristling with highbrow western intellectuals who knew all the theory about how to relieve poverty and distress, but had neither a practical interest in the villagers nor any understanding of their real needs.

To cheer her up, George and I bought her some space cookies and shoved her on a bus to the Amber Palace, thirteen clicks out of Jaipur. Amy was so blissed out by the sight of the high yellow fort, glowing ethereally bright on top of its rocky ridge, that she started shouting, 'Geooorge! I wanna _palace!_ A palace with _elephants_ in it!'

Our rickshaw driver shot her a look of alarm, ground the vehicle to a halt, and ran off somewhere, presumably to hide.

Later on, still tranced out on bhang cakes, Amy boarded another bus to a different slum project in the middle of nowhere, never to be seen again. Pity about that – my beard was just growing back.

To cheer _me_ up, George showed me a fat Italian he'd collected in the market called Ferruchio. This guy was wearing just a _lunghi_—a piece of patterned cloth wrapped round his waist—and he had about as much command of the English language as an Eskimo.

George introduced him to me, saying:

'Ferruchio. This is Frank. Say hello to Frank.'

There was a long pause, and then Ferruchio leant forward and said haltingly:

'Hey....Fraaaaaank!...COUNTRYMAN!'

'Is that IT?' I whispered to George. 'Where do you *find* these people?'

'I....Yoooou.....NEETY-GREETY-DIRT-BUNT!' followed up Ferucchio, and George gave a pleased grin.

'That's his favourite group—the Nitty Gritty Dirt Band! He must like you!'

But then Ferruchio simply ran out of English.

'Emm....you know...uh, uh....sometime you like to....ah...ah...*FUCK?*' he suggested brightly.

'This guy is not going to last long in India, is he?' I told George, but George did not agree. 'Of course he is!' he snorted. 'Indians just love mad people. They're already stroking his head and touching his lunghi for good luck. By next week, he'll probably be a plastic god inside a video bus!'

George and I had dinner that night at Gopal's Rainbow Rooftop Restaurant, sharing a table with a couple of Canadian vegetarians who spent the whole meal toying suspiciously with their mushrooms. Their hesitation wasn't actually their fault— after they'd ordered their meal, George had informed them that the local mushrooms were filled with bacteria and were not to be trusted. He had this thing about vegetarians, did George. He just loved to wind them up.

As we waited for dessert, George passed on a philosophical nugget which the Colonel had shared with him in Jaipur.

'What is more important in life,' the Colonel had mused, 'than the relationships one makes?'

'I thought that was brilliant,' said George, 'and so true!'

Around midnight, just as I was preparing to go to bed, there was a loud knocking at my door. It was George again, and he had with him a curvy young lass called Hella from Greenland. She was even more lacking in English than Ferruchio had been, but she made up for it with a big grin and a fun personality.

'Whaddaya mean, you're going to bed?' ranted George, barging into my digs. 'It's a Full Moon, man! Time to party!'

The party kicked off with a bottle of Tequila and a couple of joints, then moved on to a game of stud poker with a bunch of metal ankle-chains as the stakes. By the end, all three of us were totally wasted and our fingers were black with kerosene from the oxidised chains. Nobody even saw the Full Moon, let alone celebrated it. The last thing I remember was George and Hella staggering off to find another bottle of duty-free.

In the morning, I woke up in the same chair, fighting yet another hangover. George—incredibly and infuriatingly cheerful—burst into the room and informed me he had a new trolley man. Every buyer in town, I knew, needed a trolley man to wheel their goods from the shops to their hotel room, and George had recently sacked his old one for getting drunk. In his place now stood Baru.

Mendu had put George onto Baru, saying, 'You give him anything, he don't care. But you must watch him, because he push your things in the lake.'

'Baru is crazy,' George admitted. 'I put some goods on his trolley the other day and he headed down the road three steps at a time, inventing a new song at each stop. First came *gori gori gori*, which means *girl, girl, girl,* and then *iggy jiggy jiggy jah*, and then *eee eee eee eee*.'

It was only when George mentioned the last song that I finally placed Baru. Spud had used him the year before. Spud had thought the 'eee eee eee eee' was the sound of the trolley wheels squeaking, but he had found out different when Baru materialised in his room one night—waiting for his tip—still singing this spooky little song.

Speaking of Spud, he returned from Jaipur a few days later, complaining bitterly.

'Two jeeps were a *fuck* of a bad idea,' he informed me. 'The lead jeep had me and half our goods, and a non-English-speaking driver whose entire conversation consisted of "Me Muslim!" The other jeep carried the rest of the stuff along with every living relative of the other driver. He took us on a tour of Rajasthan, dropping people off at various points, while "Me Muslim" crawled along waiting for him to catch up. It was supposed to be a three-hour trip. Wanna know how long it took?'

I nodded.

'Six. Double the time. The entire trip I was worried about reaching Jaipur before a) Gordhan shut his shop, and b) the Arya Niwas hotel gave my room away.'

'But you made it in the end.'

'Oh yeah, I made it all right,' Spud grumbled. 'Though the Arya Niwas is going downhill fast. It's become a refugee centre for middle-class English people who are trying to escape from the rest of India. Everyone's too frightened to go outside the hotel. They've been to Delhi and they didn't like it, so they've gone to Jaipur and booked into the Arya Niwas. Now they're thinking, "Well, this is nice – croquet on the lawn and buttered scones for tea, mater!" – and they just stay there without setting a foot outside.'

I shook my head. 'I don't think that's entirely true. Some of them do get out. I've seen them.'

'Oh, you mean people like Derek the Gardener?' scoffed Spud. 'I met *him*. He had "Mr Victim" written all over him. He only came to India because he was a landscape gardener in Wigan and wanted to see the famous 17th century gardens in Kashmir. So he paid lots of money to go up there, only to be told, "This is prohibited area. You cannot see gardens on your own. You must have guide and taxi." So he paid this Kashmiri a ridiculous 500 dollars to drive him round these seven Mughal gardens for a week.

'But the first day out, they were all closed for a national holiday, and the driver says, "On the way home, I need some shopping." He stops somewhere and loads up the whole taxi— from the boot right the way to the back of Derek's head—with coal. So the next day they drive out again and the driver suddenly announces, "We cannot go this way, we must make detour." And they end up at a village where the driver starts *selling* coal. Derek couldn't believe it. He started shouting at him in broad Yorkshire, "You *bas*-tard! I've paid five hundred fooking dollars for this fooking taxi, and you're using it to sell fooking *coal?*"'

Spud shook his head, chuckling. 'Yeah,' he concluded. 'I saw him going outside the Arya Niwas, but only to check plane fares back to Wigan.'

The following morning, over breakfast, Spud met George for the first time. To my astonishment, the two short, stroppy individuals took to each other instantly. The reason? All they ever talked about was business.

'How did you guys get on with Girish?' asked George. 'Man, he's really hard work. Won't budge at all on prices.'

'That's where you need a partner,' Spud said, grinning. 'We always do the double-act on Girish. I hit him on a technicality, and Frank hits him on the price. He can't take us both at once!'

'Yeah,' I said, 'he hates it when we gang up on him. "I tell it to the Koo-see!" he protests when Spud complains about something and "I tell it to the takala!" when I start moaning. In the end, he just loses it completely and starts shouting: "I am only one man! I am not six arms and eight legs!"'

Waiting for us downstairs was my old friend Ram. I had bought Ram, a handicapped local with both legs paralysed, three camels a few years before, and had set him up in business – with an office just below the Pushkar Palace.

Ram was happy to see me again, but was suffering from a 'monkey problem'. A large red-bottomed monkey had just run off with one of his crutches and he was stranded at reception, unable to retrieve it. Norath, one of the waiters, had to pay five rupees to get it back. That was how much the bananas cost to coax the monkey off the rooftop.

'If I had to change places with anyone in Pushkar,' Spud mused, 'it would be with the Monkey King of the Rooftops. In my next life, I'm coming back as him.'

'Why's that, then?' I asked.

'Because all the female monkeys raid the market for vegetables, and every time they bring him a cauliflower they're rewarded with a shag. I watched him last time I was here, and in any one hour that monkey gets an average of four and a half shags!'

Later on, in the Om Shiva Cafe, we all hooked up with Ram again. The crutch-bound camel-man was looking rather grand this evening, wearing ruby-encrusted earrings, a richly-tapestried waistcoat, and an expensive, rainbow turban. He was also sporting a huge black beard with curled and waxed mustachios.

Something, however, was not quite right. Ram was as good-natured as ever, nodding and smiling in all the right places, but he seemed strangely removed from the conversation. Especially when Spud was talking. At the end of a very long monologue from Spud in which he described his humble origins in Ireland, his short stint in the army, his long struggle to establish himself as a plumber in south London, and his lucky inheritance of a market stall from his eldest sister, Ram just looked at him and said, *'Whut?'*

Yes, Ram had not understood one word Spud had said. Spud spoke too fast for him, it seemed, and he mumbled his English. Mortified, Spud started to repeat his story at a snail's pace, but soon gave up. Ram's beatific, uncomprehending smile was getting on his nerves. To remove that smile, Spud viciously remarked that Ram's new beard was 'pretentious'.

Ram simply nodded and said, 'thank you.'

'Actually,' I quietly informed Spud, 'Ram doesn't give two figs what you think of his beard. All he's interested in is becoming Mister Desert in Jaiselmer's forthcoming Camel Fair. He believes the only reason he didn't win the title last year was that he was the only contestant without a beard.'

George frowned, puzzled. 'Why does he have to be Mister Desert?'

'Oh, don't you know? Ram got picked out of the crowd last month by Patrick Swayze and landed a bit part in the film, *City of Joy*. After that, everybody expects him to be Mister Desert. He's so famous now he doesn't have anywhere else to go!'

₹

Chapter 12

Ram, Ram, the Camel Man

Back in my room, I told Spud and George the full story of Ram-ji or 'brother Ram'. When he and I had first met three years before, back in 1989, he hadn't been famous at all. In fact, he was a social pariah, constantly being shuffled along by local policemen. Even his own father wouldn't speak to him.

I had been introduced to Ram by Maria, my then girlfriend, who had said, 'I've just been speaking to this guy. Go and talk to him. He's special.' She was right. Ram's English wasn't good, but there was a certain something—his aura of steely determination perhaps—that made me want to help him.

The thing that had most impressed me about Ram was that he didn't want help. And that, in India, made him a rarity. He was a beautiful man, with warm moist eyes, a winning smile, and charming innocence. He was also a fierce Rajput, far too proud to beg. On first contact he was seething with rage. His fury was not so much directed against policemen (though he detested them), but at the bad cards fate had dealt him. For despite his education and obvious intelligence, he could not get a job or expect a good marriage. A doctor had given him a bad injection when he was a child and he had contracted polio. Now, he was crippled in both legs and had to get around on crutches.

'I know you don't want help,' I had said, 'but if there was one thing you could do that wouldn't require the use of your legs, what would it be?'

Ram, after lengthy consideration, replied: 'Well, I can ride *camel!*'

And so 'Ram's Desert Experience', Pushkar's very first camel-trek company was born. The deal was simple. I bought Ram three camels (total cost £100). In return Ram took me and my friends for free treks into the desert whenever we hit town. It was the only way Ram would accept my 'charity.'

I had no doubt that Ram would be successful. Pushkar was surrounded by mile upon mile of golden sand dunes all the way to Pakistan. And since every western guidebook was busy directing travellers to Jaiselmer for camel treks—not Pushkar—Ram would have no competition.

For his part, Ram saw me as an answer to a prayer. After so much bad luck in his life, he had come to Pushkar that particular day to implore Brahma, the god of the Lake, for some divine sign of favour. And I, apparently, had been it.

Brahma, Ram informed me, was one of the three main deities of the Hindu religion. He was the Creator of the universe and, together with Vishnu the Preserver and Shiva the Destroyer, represented the three basic processes in human existence: birth, life, and death. Unlike the other two deities, however, Brahma had only one temple in India, and it was right here in Pushkar.

'Brahma come, Brahma make world, Brahma go away,' explained Ram.

Hindus didn't have much faith in an absent god.

Ram, however, along with a steady trickle of pilgrims into Pushkar, placed a lot of faith in Brahma. Brahma was the guy you prayed to if you wanted something new in your life (a child, a house, a spouse). And what Ram wanted more than anything in the world was a completely new life, a life in which he was not judged by his disability but by his merits as a human being.

According to Ram, Pushkar was 'extra special' to Brahma. The legend went that a lotus blossom *(pushpa)* once fell from the hand *(kar)* of Brahma while he was searching for a place to perform his purification ritual *(yagna)*, and in the spot where it landed a lake sprang up. But having made Pushkar his home, Brahma had made the huge mistake of upsetting his wife, Savatri, by getting a substitute bride, Gayatri, to help him bless his new temple. Gayatri was an untouchable, an outcast, and in order to make her holy she was, in Ram's words, 'put into the mouth of a cow and removed from the anus'. Drastic, but apparently effective.

When Brahma's wife, Savitri, finally appeared, she was not amused. So not amused, in fact, that she placed a curse on Brahma. 'Take Pushkar!' she said. 'It's yours! But it's the only home you'll ever have!'

With this, she stormed up a hill behind the lake and had been sulking up there ever since. Brahma tried to cheer her up with a temple of her own, right at the top of the hill, but – as Ram reliably informed me – she still wasn't happy.

Ram and I crawled up to see her, a painfully slow hike up a 2000 year old stone stairway, and came upon a small white structure offering spectacular panoramic views over the lake below. Before us, way down below, lay the tiny town of Pushkar and its holy lake, while to the rear, the white, undulating sands stretched as far as the eye could see. When we'd had our fill of the spectacle, I helped Ram back down across the dunes so we could visit the Brahma temple itself.

This was a bright Disneyish effort – a riot of blue, green, yellow, and red paint, topped with a pink dome. The temple was immaculately clean and sat within a small enclosure, backing directly onto the desert. Ram pointed out the *hans* (goose) symbol of Brahma engraved above the entrance, as well as Brahma's animal carrier: a small silver turtle. As the day drew to a close, the sun hanging low in the purple sky, we walked to the rear of the temple for picture-postcard views of the desert as well as of the high Savitri Temple we had just ascended.

It had been a special day. A surreal kind of pilgrimage during which two men from completely different worlds and backgrounds forged a friendship that would change their lives forever.

*

The next morning Spud and I rolled out of town, bound for Jaipur. We'd had our short break and were looking forward to going home and cashing in our goods.

'Fuck me!' gloated Spud. 'We might become rupee millionaires sooner than we thought!'

But when we returned to London in March 1992, we hit a full-blown recession. Somehow, during our short six week absence, the whole of the UK had been gripped by the worst financial crisis since the war. Banks, offices, and shops were closing down daily, and as a sign of the times only four of the thirty market stalls at St Martin's were still operational.

'This is serious,' I said, battling panic. 'I hope to God that Liberty's still wants their bedspreads. Half our money is tied up with their order.'

Spud's entire head turned purple. 'They'd *better* want it,' he said grimly, 'or I'm going to torch the place!'

But Liberty's reneged on the deal.

'We still want the stuff,' stuttered their top buyer, flushed with apology, 'but in the current economic climate, we simply can't afford it.'

Spud's particular shade of purple darkened. 'What do you mean you can't afford it?' he raged. 'We've just travelled thousands of miles and spent thousands of pounds on your say-so, so you'd better afford it, or I'm going to stuff each of these fucking bedspreads up your arse!'

The buyer went white with shock and pressed the alarm button.

'Come away, mate,' I suggested. 'There'll be swarms of security guards here in a minute. We don't need the hassle.'

With two tons of old embroidery lying around unclaimed, and with no money to pay for its storage, I was forced to leave home. On Spud's insistence, I finally stopped living with my mother in Enfield and bought a house (which I could ill-afford) close to Spud in Peckham – a house that instantly became a warehouse, full of Dexion shelving to accommodate the vast surplus of imported goods.

The only good thing about the recession, the one thing that saved us from disaster, was the influx of rich Americans looking for cheap breaks in London. One such American, the owner of a large textile gallery in New York, turned up at St Martin's market and spotted one of Damoder's beautiful old bedspreads hanging up behind my stall.

'Gee!' she exclaimed. 'The folks back home will *eat* this stuff up! Have you got any *more?*' I promptly marched her over to Peckham and sold her every piece I had, and at a far better price than Liberty's had offered. Even Spud was impressed.

'Nice one!' he said happily. 'One day bank-rupert, the next quids-in!'

'No thanks to you,' I thought sourly. I was coming around to the opinion that—just like the Colonel in Jaipur—the bigger Spud's plans got, the more likely they were to end in disaster, and the more likely I would be left to mop things up. Yes, we had been lucky this time. But what if it happened again?

₹

Chapter 13

Recession? What Recession?

Many businesses fold or at least cut back in the face of a recession. Spud decided to expand.

'It's a golden opportunity,' he told me. 'Nobody else has been buying in India, so nobody else will have stock.'

The fact that nobody had money to buy more stock never occurred to him. I shook my head, bemused. 'We've already got two whole houses bulging with stuff. How do you intend to sell it?'

Spud pointed out of his kitchen window, indicating a shiny new van. 'I'm going to invade England. That's how!'

His plan, as far as I could make out, was to wholesale to every hippy shop in the country.

'Okay,' argued Spud when I frowned, 'we'll make far less money wholesaling. Less than half of what we made in the markets. But think of it this way: we'll turn over far more stuff in far less time. Anything we have left we'll punt out to the festivals in the summer.'

With that he was gone. The big new van rolled out of his driveway one morning and didn't return for a month. During that time, the only news I had of him were the frequent phone calls I got from shops that Spud had terrorised.

Spud had a unique sales technique, I discovered: fast and furious. Upon entering any new town or city, he drove slowly around it, scouting any possible shops which might buy his products. Once he located the biggest one he barged into it, informing the reluctant owner, 'If you don't buy off me, I'll just go up the road and sell to someone else.'

This was the last thing they wanted to hear, of course, so he got his foot in the door. If they still refused to entertain him, he stayed exactly where he was. He stood in front of the counter looking manic—one arm full of clothing and the other full of jewellery—until all the customers had fled and the owner nervously enquired, 'So what have you got then?' It was as close to bullying as Spud could get without being arrested.

I didn't have a sales technique. I was content behind my stall, serving people who actually wanted something, and I didn't want to impose myself on reluctant shopkeepers. Spud found this very frustrating.

'I've got this partner, Frank,' he told one client in Folkestone, 'and I've been trying for two years to get him to enter any shop, which he refuses to do. So I've made all the contacts, and he's made none. I can't seem to drag him off his bloody market stall!'

Later on, when I *did* go wholesaling, the same client told me: 'We were so glad when you turned up. Spud was a sweaty little thug. He flogged us these huge silk shorts, saying: "They're very popular with big women because it stops their fat thighs chafing against each other." We only bought some so we could get rid of him!'

Spud collected shops like some people collect postage stamps. He had a map of Britain on his office wall, and he stuck pins in it every time he returned from a fresh scouting party. A fierce army of one, he first attacked London, then the

South Coast, then Wales and the West Country, and finally the Midlands and the North. Like the Romans of old, he got as far as Hadrian's Wall and stopped just short of invading Scotland.

By now, around the end of 1992, he had over two hundred shops to sell to—like two hundred little occupational castles— and finally proclaimed himself satisfied. Of course sustaining this far-flung empire was too much for Spud to do alone. He began employing agents to sell for him, and he bought a fleet of vans for the purpose. The biggest shops, the ones who spent the most money and kept the whole thing afloat, he saved for me.

Spud discovered I was his best salesman quite by accident. One late night in 1992 he was due to drive down West for a whole week's wholesaling, but he couldn't drive anywhere that night due to a swollen testicle.

'I'm genitally disadvantaged,' he woke me to say, 'so you're going to have to do all my calls this week.'

I wasn't happy. I hated driving, especially at night, and I had never been behind the wheel of Spud's giant delivery van before. I also had no experience at wholesaling, and didn't know if I would be any good at it. I grudgingly set out at 3am, sleepy-headed, heavy-hearted, and terrified of motorways.

I needn't have worried. The first shop, in Bournemouth, invited me in and went through my van while I slept upstairs in their 'Lama room'. They only woke me up to stuff a cheque for two grand in my hand.

'Well, that was easy,' I thought. 'Maybe I can do this job after all!'

Turns out the shop had been so grateful that Spud hadn't turned up, they had bought twice as much stuff as usual. And it was the same everywhere I went. My negative salesmanship— the fact that I didn't seem to want to sell anybody anything—

was so opposite to Spud's approach that I was an immediate success.

This trip was my first time off a market stall in over two years, and I surprised myself by really enjoying it. The people I met were so friendly it didn't even seem like work. But when I phoned Spud to tell him of my Bournemouth success I was tersely deflated.

'You only saw one shop?' he grumbled. 'How are you going to fit the other *twelve* in?'

I slammed down the receiver.

The next day, Tuesday, I drove lazily down to Taunton. Unlike Spud, who blitzed through at least six shops a day, I drifted into one, had a leisurely chat with the owners for an hour or two, shared a nice lunch with them, and only got round to talking business around 3pm.

'At this rate,' I thought to myself, 'I'll be lucky to see six shops in a week!'

Spud thought the same thing and was mad as hell. 'If you got up earlier,' he shouted down the phone, 'you could squeeze in three shops before lunch! Why don't you do what I do?'

'Because I'm not an insomniac like you!' I shouted back. 'And anyway, I'm making more money from one shop than you do from six! Why don't you spend more time with your customers? Then they might buy more from you!'

On the Wednesday, I travelled from the West Country up to Wales and saw three shops in quick, pleasant succession.

'In our business,' I noted in my diary, 'being *liked* by one's customers is pretty important. Every shop I've seen so far has been 'alternative' and anti-establishment. They don't like salesmen with suits and briefcases, or even ties. They like relaxed, non-pushy people who have obviously been to Asia and who dress down for the occasion. They don't blink an eye when I turn up in a tie-dye hat or a grungy old pair of ripped jeans. They also like my mud-splattered van and for everything in it to be all over the place, not in nicely arranged plastic boxes. In short, they like to plunge into a chaos of stock and have a jolly good rummage. Something else they like—and Spud will never get his head round this one—is to chew the fat for at least an hour before even bringing up the subject of business. It's a virtual family, this small band of new-age shops and their respective wholesalers, and it is important that we exchange lives and laughs, that they feel I've come just as much to see *them* as to sell them stuff. I've only met these people once, but already, because of the same "language" we speak, I can see them becoming long-term friends.'

I liked Wales, so I stayed an extra day. I had been to university there, and I still fondly recalled its beautiful scenery and kindly inhabitants. For two years out of three it had rained, but in humour and disposition Wales reminded me of one other country: India.

Even the Welsh police were nice. I got pulled over by a squad car that morning as I attempted to find my way to Swansea. They wanted to know what I was doing, driving at 80 miles an hour, rolling a fag with my elbows on the wheel, and looking at a map set between my legs instead of watching the road.

'I'm lost,' I told them haplessly. 'Can you give me directions?' To my surprise, they did.

In Swansea, the shopkeeper, a dapper little gent named John, insisted I sing some Welsh hymns with him. In exchange, he bought exactly one hundred of everything he liked and nothing of what he didn't like. The Welsh, I recalled, were fairly superstitious.

John then put me on to a new shop, 'Equinox' in Tenby, to

whom he himself wholesaled.

'You'll do well there, boyo,' he informed me. 'It's a cracker. The biggest shop in Wales!'

I limped into Tenby around dusk, my gearbox shot to pieces. Only the first and third gears were still intact, and I couldn't find reverse. Megan and Philip, the owners of Equinox, were very helpful. While I rang the AA for assistance, they went through my van and bought practically all of its contents. Then, as the van was towed away to a nearby garage, they took me out for a slap-up meal and put me up overnight.

The following morning, while my new gearbox was being fitted, my new friends gave me a guided tour of Tenby, a cosy little seaside spot with perhaps the best beach in Wales. One of the Georges (George the Third?) had converted this into a popular bathing spa in the 18th century, and it still retained many of its original features, including cobbled backstreets, pastel buildings, seafaring inns and quaint nook-and-cranny bookshops. It was easy to see why Equinox did so well. It was the biggest "alternative" shop in Wales, offering four floors of goodies from all around the world.

There was no need to linger longer – I had nothing left to sell. So as soon as I got my van back from the garage, I returned to London without stopping. Along the way, I wondered what Spud was making such a fuss about. This wholesaling business was a piece of cake. All that was required, I reflected, was to work out what my customers wanted—which might include anything from doing their horoscopes to singing Gaelic hymns—and give it to them. It was an act—a performance if you like – but as long as I managed to stay cheerful and look interested throughout, they seemed to forget the recession and plied me with friendship and lots of money.

Spud couldn't believe the size of the cheques I brought home. Especially the massive cheque from Tenby. 'You haven't been selling on the cheap again, have you?' he asked suspiciously.

'Of course not,' I lied glibly. I lied because Spud couldn't have taken the truth, which was that nobody liked either him or his high prices, and I had been giving generous discounts. Especially to 'Equinox' for paying up front, rather than waiting the standard thirty days. I was confident in the lie, too. Spud had lost patience with stocktaking. He no longer had any idea of what was in his van or what it was worth.

But my lie promptly backfired. Spud whisked me off my beloved market stall in St Martin's, replaced me with a cute little redhead named Anita, and sent me wholesaling fulltime. From then on, Spud only visited new shops once. After that, very shrewdly, he sent me in to 'make friends' with them.

*

A month or so later we were at Glastonbury, the biggest rock festival in England. Every freak, hippy, groupie, and eco-warrior in the country came to this place in June to rock on, space out, and jump up and down to bands they couldn't remember in the morning. We had pitched here, Spud and I, twice before, but this time we had come to wholesale to other stalls who couldn't afford, in the current economic climate, to go to India themselves.

This particular Glastonbury, ironically, spelt the beginning of the end of our partnership. We were at the peak of our powers, at the very top of our game. We had seventeen market stalls in and around London, were wholesaling to hundreds of shops nationwide, doing all the major festivals, and presenting at the most prestigious shows and fairs. We had become rupee millionaires several times over, and Spud speculated that we were single-handedly setting the youth fashion for the whole of the UK.

It was too good to last, and it began to fall apart for the most trivial of reasons.

We had finished our business, attended to all our customers in the Green Field, and I was bored. I gathered up a pile of useless trinkets, mainly cheap bead bracelets, and threw down a blanket at the entrance to the main Pyramid stage. Here, donning a headscarf and a ratty old T-shirt, I posed as an itinerant hippy and began fly-pitching.

Business was slow to start with. I'd never sold to the masses before and felt intimidated with the process, but it picked up massively with the arrival of Dwell. Dwell was a freak in every sense of the word. He was extremely stoned, he wore nothing but a loincloth, and he had covered himself in ash and mud in order to look like a tree. His deal was a wheelbarrow full of melons which he had purchased somewhere for fifty pence each. He cut each melon into sixteen pieces and sold each piece for a quid.

'So what's with the name?' I asked, making room for him on my blanket.

'Iss my name, innit.'

'No, why do you call yourself Dwell?'

There was a long pause, as Dwell considered the question. 'Because that's what I *do*, man,' he said at last. 'Dwell!'

Over the next hour, as the sun rose high in the sky and everyone became melon (and trinket) happy, Dwell and I filled our pockets with more cash, booze, and drugs than we knew what to do with.

Then a couple of security guards came over. 'You shouldn't be here,' warned the first. 'If you're still here when we come back, we'll confiscate your stuff.'

'That's right,' said the second with a wink. 'But give us a melon to slow us up a bit.'

An hour later they were back. This time there was no discussion. They ripped up my blanket with its few remaining trinkets inside, and marched off with it.

'Please don't take that, man!' I moaned after them. 'That's all I got left in the world!'

Dwell and I exchanged a secret smirk. I had a whole vanload of stuff left, if I cared to use it, and he had a back-up wheelbarrow full of melons.

Returning to the van, glowing with triumph, I found Spud unexpectedly miffed. 'Anyone can do that!' snorted Spud. 'Watch and learn!'

With that he vanished, his bald pate covered in a rasta wig of rainbow string chokers. He was gone a long time too, as he tried to sell the chokers off his head for £5 each. But nobody wanted them - he was too pushy, the price was too high – and he returned in a major sulk. In his mind, *he* was the salesman, not me. And he had just been shown up as a rank amateur.

To put things right, to show me who was boss, he 'accidentally' locked me in the van that night, forcing me to piss into two empty beer cans. The following morning, shortly after I was released, I was horrified to see two drunks fighting over those two cans, thinking they were fresh lager.

As the sun came up, and the wheel of karma turned, Spud found himself equally horrified. The van was now surrounded by a field full of cats, vegetarians, and astrologers, the three things he hated most in the world. One particular couple sitting just below the van finally pushed him over the edge.

'My cat's a vegetarian!' remarked one of them, to which the other replied, 'That's nothing. My cat's an Aquarian vegetarian. He's born the same day as Ronald Reagan!'

'That's *it!'* declared Spud and stormed off to the bridge below the Green Field to score some drugs. He returned soon after with a big smile on his face and an even bigger rock of cocaine between his teeth. That was the first time I saw Spud do drugs.

It was the stress, I guessed, the non-stop grind of work and business, that was getting to him. Plus the growing realisation that pots of money hadn't made him the babe magnet he had expected. He was a rupee millionaire, sure, but still no woman liked him.

Spud was due a trip back to India. He needed to see a country where people could be happy with no money just to restore his perspective. But sending him there was easier said than done. He didn't want to go.

'You fly ahead,' he told me, 'and I'll follow on in a week or so.'

I should have questioned his motives, but I didn't and that was a bad mistake.

Little did I know it, but Spud was starting to crack up.

₹

Chapter 14

The Pushkar Posse

I flew back to Delhi on 10th September 1993. It was the tail-end of the monsoons, and while the temperature was only 25 degrees, it was still very humid. The sultry weather matched my mood. Just before flying, Spud – still smarting from his humiliation at Glastonbury – had suddenly turned on me.

'What the fuck are these?' he demanded with a sneer, poking with distaste at the five hundred *dolki* bags that had just arrived from India.

'They're dolki bags,' I replied. 'You wear them as shoulder bags. And look, there's a drawstring at the top with tinkly bells on it. All the kids wear them in Pushkar.'

Spud gave a hollow laugh. 'Oh yeah,' he said, 'and I suppose they'll "go a bomb" at our markets. Just like those three hundred floppy hats you bought last year, the ones which are still sitting in my closet!'

I was confused. Spud had never questioned my buying decisions before. It was an unspoken rule that I was in charge of the buying and he of the selling. Even when the damn dolki bags had sold, the day before I flew, they remained the subject of barbed and sarcastic comments.

'How much did you punt them out for?' Spud asked,

glaring. 'Tuppence each?'

I let that one go with difficulty. Spud couldn't help it, I reasoned to myself. The business was escalating so fast he was hardly sleeping at all. And the more he drove himself, the more grumpy and bad-tempered he was becoming. Little things were getting to him—little things like the dolki bags— and they were assuming disproportionate importance. But I was rapidly running out of excuses for Spud. One day soon the tightly stretched elastic of my patience would just snap.

I was a careful buyer. I knew the way forward was beads – cheap Tibetan beads. That's what had sold so well during my first year on the markets. That was also what had netted me over a grand at Glastonbury.

Without telling Spud, who was conveniently absent, I stopped in Delhi at the bead centre of the capital: the Old Tibetan Market of Janpath. Here I found my old friend, Pema, working in a shop called Tibetan Arts. Always calm and serene, his round moon face fixed in a beatific smile, Pema was the most laidback person I had ever met. He was wholly unflappable. Even when I laid five grand worth of rupees on him and said, 'Can you make me 20,000 bead pieces in ten days?' he barely twitched a muscle.

'I will make it,' he said, then returned to contemplating the cockroach on his desk.

My business complete, I returned to my hotel and dashed off a letter to Spud, telling him to truck this massive order of beads to Jaipur when he finally flew in from England.

'Don't take the bus,' I wrote urgently. 'There's far too much of it, and they won't let you on.'

I was speaking from experience. A few trips earlier I had tried to stuff the entire back boot of the bus to Jaipur with something like three thousand of Pema's bone bracelets. That hadn't worked. There hadn't been room for anyone else's luggage.

The following morning I travelled down to Paharganj to meet up with American George, who was hanging out at the dingy but friendly Major's Den. The Major's Den was located just off Main Bazar and was run by a genial old gentleman whom everyone—including his much younger wife—simply referred to as "the Major." George liked the Den because it was cheap, clean, and full of young hippy chicks to whom he could play his ukulele.

Despite his strict army training, the Major was tolerance incarnate. George was allowed to drink, smoke blow, and entertain girls as much as he liked, without the slightest reproach. This was partly because the Major liked Americans, but mainly because George fussed endlessly over the old man's baby daughter, who had been born—much to the Major's surprise—after twenty years of marriage ...and with him just planning on a wheelchair.

When I arrived, the Major was sitting outside his lodge, his daughter on one knee and the *Times of India* on the other. He was wearing his familiar blue blazer and ironed slacks, and he peered at me quizzically through his thick spectacles until recognition dawned.

'Ah, my good chap!' he croaked benignly. 'How good to see you! Mister George is on the roof.'

Mister George was indeed on the roof, and he had a new friend: an impish little ruffian named Lal, whom George had plucked out of an alleyway off Janpath. Lal was seven years old, and his parents were dead. The little boy spent his working days crouched between two taxi cabs outside Palika Bazar, shovelling dollops of green slime onto the shiny new shoes of passing tourists so that his chum, located twenty yards further up the road, could charge them ten rupees for a shoeshine. It really was a great scam, and George had brought Lal up here so he could write a song about it. Fortunately, it was a very short song: 'Lal is my pal, but check your shoes, for doggy doos …'

The next day, George and I rode a deluxe bus bound for Pushkar. I had suggested a taxi instead, but George had been outraged at the idea.

'No *way!*' he'd howled petulantly. 'Going down National Highway number 8 in a taxi is equivalent to a speck of dust trying to get through an asteroid belt!'

He had a point. Highway 8 was the most dangerous stretch of road in India – over 1000 kilometres of dead straight tarmac, all the way from Delhi to Bombay, with all three lanes occupied by speed-crazed lorries trying to overtake each other. Most taxis spent half their time bouncing along the hard shoulder, hoping to get access to the actual highway.

While George fell asleep in the back of the bus, I examined his outfit, noting that my strange American friend had now got his 'world traveller' apparel down to a fine art. His compact munchkin figure wore a short-cropped jeans jacket from Nepal over a ratty pink T-shirt he'd picked up in Bangkok which was decorated with the simple message, 'Fuck You.' Beneath a pair of worn out, fashionably torn Levis from Dharamsala poked a brace of dusty hiking boots obtained second-hand from a hill porter in Manali. All this was topped by an expandable Afghani hat, into which he tucked his long, matted dreadlocks.

As for his bespectacled features, these were rendered quite dwarfish by a wispy little beard, cut short at the cheeks and running wild below the chin. A glittering array of chunky ethnic rings adorned each finger. He actually had an extra one—fortunately out of sight—which had been inserted into his penis during his last foray into Paharganj. Around his neck hung a final touch: a valuable Zzi-bead necklace purchased from a Tibetan family in Ladakh for the considerable sum of 1600 dollars. Nobody looking at him would have guessed that this was the foremost wholesaler of hippy goods into America.

For the next six hours George was totally comatose. Having pulled out his bus ticket so it protruded slightly from the top pocket of his jacket—thus preventing the conductor from waking him—he propped himself up so his head rested on a three-kilo bag of silver he'd bought in Delhi. A beatific smile played across his lips, suggestive of a pleasant end to his night with the silent Norwegian.

When he finally came to, five minutes from Jaipur, he made a profound (for him) comment. 'You're much more fun on your own, Frank. Why don't you dump that motherfucker?'

'Who? You mean Spud?'

'Yeah, I mean Spud. You've been bitching and complaining about him ever since we hooked up. Why don't you just cut him loose?'

It was a good question, and one for which I had no easy answer.

'Well, there's two things,' I said at last. 'First, he's the driving force behind my business. Without him, I'd still be sitting on a market stall selling nose-studs. Second, and more importantly, he knows where I live.'

'Oh man, come on. You really think he'd trash your place like he did Ivan's landlord?'

'I don't think it. I know it.'

George gave a deep sigh. 'You guys sound like an old married couple. Why don't you get a trial separation or somethin'?'

I thought of Lou. Somehow, I didn't think Spud did trial separations.

Safely back in Pushkar, I left George to recover in his room while I strolled into the market. Here I made three new friends. First there was Susie, a chirpy Cockney girl I found trying to decide between two pairs of socks. Then there was Nick and Anna, the friendly couple I bumped into at the Payal Guest House while I was trying to score some charas.

Nick was a blonde, blue-eyed Liverpudlian who had come to Pushkar to buy silk for his market stall in Vancouver, where Anna lived. The couple had first met at a rave party in London, and it was a match made in heaven. They could not have been more different—yet more alike. Nick was the quiet one, with a wild quiff of hair and a penchant for magic tricks. Anna was the chatty, smiley one, all sweet and innocent; a real child of nature. What bound them together was a love of travel, and of India in particular. Unlike me, they didn't stay at big hotels or eat at fancy restaurants. They experienced India at a grassroots level. The more down and dirty it got, the more they seemed to like it. And they never spoke English when Hindi would do. Anna never asked, 'One tea, please?' when she could ask, 'ek chai, milega?' Nick carried round an ancient Hindi phrasebook containing useful instructions like 'mind your own business' and 'catch that rat.'

I first met Nick on the roof of the Payal, playing with festooned devil sticks. We immediately hit it off.

'You gotta read this book, Frank!' he enthused. 'It's called *Hindustani Without A Master*, and it's packed with hilarious phrases. I've been trying some of them out in the market, and the Indians have been totally gobsmacked!'

The phrases Nick had used to greatest effect were as follows:

There are many motor cars in Bombay
I ride him every morning
My horse is warm
I intend to go to Persia
This is my monkey
The lock of your musket is rusty
A sepoy has shot himself
I had four motions
He will be hanged at dawn

I discovered Anna down below, suffering from some sort of tummy bug. As a result, she had been hassled all day long by medicine men and charlatans offering her strange 'cures'. The weirdest one, she said, was the guy who advised her to go out next Saturday afternoon at 3pm precisely, locate a black dog and pour mustard oil on its head.

That evening we all gathered at the Venus restaurant, just up from the Palace Hotel. The Venus was a new venue with the same rooftop set-up as every other hippy hangout in town, but with twinkling fairy lights on the ceiling and little balcony nooks where one could look down on the street below. I liked it because it had the best vegetarian dish in Pushkar: the 'Venus Special Thali'. Nick liked it because it had the best and worst deals of any menu in India. The best deal, which allowed him to chill out all day without actually eating anything, was lemon tea at one rupee (two pence). The worst deal, which cost him a whole rupee extra, was 'no ice' at two rupees. Whenever his lemon tea evaporated and he was in danger of being ejected, he confused the waiter into going away by ordering 'no ice.'

We all liked the Venus for its rapid rotation of crazy

waiters. The first one, whom we encountered that night, was known simply as Penis. He came from somewhere near Mathura, south of Delhi, and he had been picked up from the Ajmer bus stand by the Venus manager. The problem with Penis, and the reason he had acquired this unfortunate nickname, was that he had a lisp and couldn't get his tongue around the letter 'f'. So whenever he turned up take our dishes away, he innocently enquired 'Penis?' instead of 'Finish?' This amusing slip provoked a variety of responses, ranging from, 'No thanks, I've already got one' (me) to 'My room or yours?' (Nick). Later on, some tourist took it the wrong way and kneed poor Penis in the groin, rendering him instantly unemployable. He was back at the bus stand the next day.

₹

Chapter 15

Susie

At some point in the evening we were joined by Susie and her shy new husband, Raju. Susie and Raju were the unlikeliest couple I had ever met. She was a gobby redhead from Dagenham, about as East-End as they come, and he was a pint-sized tea boy from Pushkar with not one word of English.

'People come to India for many reasons,' Susie confided. 'To find themselves, to lose themselves, to make money, or simply to hang out. In my case, it was to forget a terrible marriage. Look at this!'

She handed me a photograph of her first wedding. I was flabbergasted. It was hard—no, it was *impossible* to reconcile the shapely young blonde on that faded photo with the emaciated, copper-headed hippy chick sitting beside me.

'Is that really you?' I exclaimed.

'Yes, before my husband cheated on me with my own sister. I had a motto back then: show me a man, and I'll show you a bastard!'

Susie had travelled to India two years before, having taken a vow of everlasting chastity. Then she met Raju, and her vow was promptly broken. In fact, she seemed to feel it important to describe—in great detail—the many ways in which it *had* been broken, and the many places. What Raju lacked in English he evidently made up for in erotic dexterity and imagination. One year later, inevitably, along came baby Om Prakash, born on the same rooftop hovel Susie called home, and spoilt rotten by all the neighbouring Indians.

Susie was happy in India. She had gone native in a way that even Nick and Anna had never managed. She cooked her own bread, rice, and vegetables, she spoke fluent Hindi with the locals (albeit in a wide-boy accent), and she wore just two changes of threadbare clothing. She had 'married' Raju in a traditional ceremony to please Indian custom, and dressed little Om Prakash in Rajasthani costumes, dotting his brow with coloured bindi spots and painting his huge, wondering eyes with black *kohl*. Now a second baby was on the way, and she was considering going back to Dagenham. She couldn't explain why, but she felt they would all be better off in the West.

The best thing about Susie, I decided, was that she was so genuine, with no pretences at all. She instantly adopted everyone around the table into her own family, dubbing us the 'Pushkar Posse' and insisting we touch base with her every time we blew into town.

The common denominator, of course, was not Susie, but Ram. Directly or indirectly, we were all taking inspiration from his innocence, his charm, and his eagerness to incorporate the values of his world with those of ours. Without him, we were just aliens on a distant planet – tolerated, welcomed even, but never entirely trusted. With him, we could form our own tribe.

The following day happened to be a Full Moon, the most fortuitous time to visit the desert, and Ram suggested what would become an annual tradition – the Full Moon Camel

Safari. He arranged for five camels to wait for us at the far side of the lake bridge—the fifth being for his very first girlfriend, a young and pretty Japanese student named Eri. I was both surprised and happy that Ram had finally found romance. I wasn't sure how Ram's family would view it, but of one thing I was certain: Eri had looked past Ram's withered legs and, like myself, she had seen the shining light within.

We set out around dusk, just as a flock of giant fruit bats took flight and sailed overhead, flapping silently from one ancient banyan tree to another. We set up camp at an old hospitality building and watched the evening sky turn a deep, velvety blue as the thin clouds burned a vivid rose-pink before fading into darkness. Night fell quickly, leaving us with no electricity, only oil lamps. A bonfire was lit, bread *rotis*, and cooked vegetables were passed around, and Ram guided us all to a rise where we were treated to an unforgettable sight: the sun setting and the moon rising at the same time. The Full Moon emerged from behind the mountains like a huge copper penny, and just hung there, glowing ethereal orange on the horizon, before slowly ascending into the heavens.

As night drew in, a troupe of local gypsy girls turned up, along with a succession of one-string fiddlers, and the assembly was entertained to an impromptu dance show. The girls, cheekily referred to by Ram as 'desert tarts', were bedecked in heavy tribal jewellery, wore colourful costumes, and ran around the fire screeching like banshees. To make the evening even more exciting, an electric storm illuminated the sky while the girls were dancing, treating us to spectacular flashes of multi-forked lightning.

Much later on, after a few bottles of triple-strength army rum, we drifted off to sleep under a canopy of stars. Sleeping out on the dunes was a magical experience. The night sky was clear, the desert silent. Bunched cacti and brush lay in stark relief to the marble-smooth sands like giant, surreal spiders frozen to the desert floor.

The sunrise, like the sunset, was another glorious spectacle. It heralded the arrival of a huge breakfast, cooked by the drivers, of traditional desert dishes and a big pot of steaming cardamom tea. After that, we took a slow, soothing ride back to Pushkar. The vista was an eerie, empty wasteland of rolling sands interspersed with bare rock and desolate scrub. From time to time Ram pointed out a *chinkara* (Indian gazelle) springing across the flatlands, or a flock of bright-plumed peacocks out for a stroll. Elsewhere we spotted the occasional fox, mongoose, or desert rat. A few hours of this and our minds switched off and began to play tricks. The most common mirage was of a five star hotel with a refrigerated pool and ice cold beers.

By this time, we had got used to the peculiar rocking-rolling sensation of camel-riding and our kidneys had had a jolly good shuffle. Then George made the mistake of complaining about an aching bum. His driver, a burnt-black individual determined to be of assistance, promptly hurled him face down on the sand and pummelled his buttocks until he screamed for mercy. Nick and Anna found this hilarious and began taking photographs. The grinning driver coaxed a humiliated George back up, then spent the rest of the trip giving him massages, both on and off the camel.

Back in Pushkar, with another sunset approaching, Ram led us all down to the lake for his 'tour finale.' As the time approached for *darshan* (putting the gods to bed), hundreds of tiny temples by the lakeside suddenly sprang to life. The air was filled with the clanging of bells, the beating of drums, and the hypnotic drone of prayer.

'For many westerners,' Susie informed us, 'this is the nearest they'll ever get to a "mystical" experience of India.'

Back in my room I reflected that I hadn't had such a good time in ages. I had finally found some likeminded people with whom I could enjoy India, fellow trader-travellers who were here for fun, not just business. It was a new experience, having real friends in India, and it made me realise what I had been missing all along.

The next step, I thought wistfully, was finding a proper girlfriend. Yes, there had been Amy, but that had just been a short, drunken interlude. The business, or rather Spud's interpretation of the business, had allowed me no romance at all except for the occasional one-night stand. And as soon as Spud got wind of things, a second night was out of the question. The most recent candidate, a pretty young stockbroker from Luton, had rung me up the day-after-the-night-before, and she had got Spud instead.

'Oh, you must be Spud!' she'd gushed with enthusiasm. 'I've heard so much about you! Frank's done my Chinese horoscope, and he says because he's the year of the Horse and I'm the year of the Tiger and you're the year of the Dog, we'll all get on famously!'

'No, we fucking won't!' grunted Spud. Then he hung up on her.

The more I thought about it, the more convinced I became that Spud didn't want me to have a girlfriend. Spud wanted me all to himself. He wasn't gay—I knew that—but he was certainly misogynist and possessive. Lou, his ex-wife, told me Spud had been so desperate to get married that he had proposed to every girl he went out with—on the very first date. The only reason she had said yes was that she had been extremely drunk at the time and caught completely off-guard.

After that, he made her life a living hell, cutting her off from her friends, sneaking off with prostitutes, and constantly criticising her weight and general appearance. She warned me that Spud could 'switch' at any moment, transforming from a psycho-genius 'funny man' to a domineering tyrant. I waved off her warnings, thinking nothing of them. I reckoned I could handle it. After all, my stepfather had been just the same: one minute friendly and avuncular, the next a volcano of verbal abuse. I had learnt early to shrug it all off.

So when Spud had one of his 'spells', like refusing me sick leave or cruelly destroying my short-lived affairs, I didn't let it affect me. I simply waited for the storm to pass, then I sat him down and quietly explained that his behaviour was unacceptable. Like the Rottweiler he was, Spud could be pacified in this way, though not for long. As soon as I let go of the leash he was off again, attacking everything in sight. It hadn't been a problem until now; I had managed to direct Spud's energies positively. But ever since the clash at Glastonbury, Lou's prediction of disaster was slowly coming true. Spud's street cred had been seriously damaged that day, and his attacks were no longer general. They were homing in on me.

The same day he trashed my dolki bags, for instance, Spud put Steve, my only friend on St Martin's market, in hospital. Steve was a juggler and hardly a day had gone past without his coming up and saying, 'Give me five minutes of your time and I'll teach you to juggle.'

I gave him a whole hour one day. At the end of it he stood in puzzlement, scratching his head. 'I don't understand it,' he muttered. 'You can't juggle.'

For some reason this had made us laugh. From then on, Steve was always on hand to man my stall for me when I got called away, or to juggle away some of my more awkward customers. The only awkward customer he couldn't juggle away was Spud. Spud found Steve on my pitch that day. When Steve asked him if he'd like to learn juggling too, Spud told him, 'If you don't fuck off right now, I'm going to hand you your balls.'

Unfortunately, Steve hadn't taken him seriously.

₹

Chapter 16

Troubles with Spud

Speaking of Spud, where was he? I hadn't heard from him in two weeks, and I was mad as hell. Not just because he wasn't in India helping me out, but because of the phone call I had just made to Tim, our assistant, in London. According to Tim, Spud had only that day flown for India and was proceeding directly on to Jaipur by train. That meant he wouldn't be staying in Delhi, he wouldn't get the message I had left him there, and he wouldn't be bringing all those beads from Pema to Gordhan for export. What that meant was that we were going to lose over a million rupees of profit.

'What a cock-up!' I fumed to myself. Spud was like a chess piece with the word 'random' pinned to it. I could no longer predict what he was going to do next.

Rather than brood on negatives, however, I began to consider alternatives. Who did I know who would do anything—even board a night bus to Delhi at the drop of a hat – to do me a favour? One name sprang to mind: Satish Agarwal.

Satish had a shop in the centre of Pushkar market. He had been supplying me with goods—mainly woollen jackets—for the past two years. The best thing about Satish, the one thing I

found most rare and touching, was that whatever I wanted—
even obscure things like rare Tibetan beads or antique
Victorian rupees—Satish would bend heaven and earth to find
them.

'Oh yes!' he would say. 'I see this thing in the village
yesterday. I will bring it!'

Half an hour later I was in Satish's shop explaining my
predicament to him, using the most desperate terms. Satish's
response was better than I'd anticipated.

'Come *on!*' he replied happily. 'What you want? I go to
Delhi. It is my *duty!*'

Within minutes he was on board a taxi bound for Pema's
shop, with a thousand dollars of my money, to collect the
stranded goods.

I waved him a grateful goodbye, wondering as I did so
what made Satish so very obliging. A couple of days earlier he
had sold me a thousand cotton shirts for less than it cost him to
make them.

'No problem,' had been his smiling response. 'Maybe you
give me better price *next* time!'

I wasn't sure about those shirts, though. I was dreading
another lecture from Spud.

*

A few days later everyone went their separate ways. Nick
and Anna headed down south to Madras, George back to the
States, Susie to Raju's village, and me to Jaipur to meet Spud.
It was time, we all agreed, to leave Pushkar. The climate had
become uncustomarily hot, and several travellers had fevers
and chills caused by sleeping sweaty under draughty fans.
Every room in town was full of cockroaches and ants, and

there was a power-cut every couple of hours.

Before leaving, I took a chance and dropped in on Ram. I hadn't seen my old friend in days and, considering the climate, I was a little concerned. I found Ram in his shop, his hair raging wildly around his head, his eyes wide.

'What happened?' I asked.

He mopped his brow, waiting to catch his breath before he explained. 'I am having very big fight with mosquito!' he panted. 'I kill them all—twenty or more—and put them in ashtray!'

Ram had only just returned from Jaiselmer, he told me. After once again missing his shot at Mister Desert, he had vanished into the dunes for two days, drinking himself stupid on desert rum. The only thing that cheered him up and made our parting positive, was when I showed him a glum passport photo of Spud.

'He look like he lose everything in business!' Ram crowed, laughing so hard he fell off his crutches.

Unfortunately, one of the crutches broke in half and Ram issued me with an interesting challenge: how to find a new one in Jaipur on a Sunday when everything was closed.

Later on, as I watched Satish's shirts being loaded onto the hotel van, I thought of Gordhan and his super efficient computer mind. If anyone knew, he would.

*

Six hours later I arrived at Gordhan's house and found Spud waiting for me. I was not happy to see him and bluntly told him so.

Confronted by my displeasure, Spud just shrugged and said: 'I received no instructions.'

Of course he hadn't. His instructions were still sitting in the lobby of the Oberoi hotel in Delhi, I told him, but the nearest I got to an apology was, 'I decided to come incognito this time.'

To Spud's credit, he had just generated £12,000 at a London show, so I couldn't be too hard on him. My only concern was the traces of white powder around his nose, and the way he kept sniffing all the time.

If I was in a bad mood, it was nothing compared to Spud's. He was hungry, he said, and he'd just learnt that his favourite restaurant in Jaipur, Niro's, was closed due to a BJP rally. He simply couldn't understand why a bunch of communists should have come along and deprived him of his long-awaited fish and chips.

His mood darkened further when Gordhan offered us lunch at his house instead. He served us rice with little green apples, which he insisted were 'not so hot.'

Several glasses of water later, I regained the power of speech and croakily enquired about his staff. 'Last time I came,' I reminded Gordhan, 'all your workers had eye flu and were wearing dark shades to stop the bug from leaping out and infecting us. They looked like hit men.'

'Yus,' laughed Gordhan. 'Pup Fikshon!

He was far less happy when I showed him Ram's broken crutch. Then he spotted an injured worker and snatched the poor man's crutch from him. 'He break leg last week,' said Gordhan carelessly. 'No need now.'

Later on, Spud and I joined Girish in his upstairs grotto and began checking his silver. We were just about finished when Spud dropped a bombshell.

'I've got to go to Thailand,' he casually informed me.
'What?'
'Oh, didn't I tell you?' he asked, innocence personified.

'I'm going to Southeast Asia on a buying trip. I've got to hop on a train in ten minutes for the airport.'

I was so stunned I didn't know what to say – just sat there in silence while Spud made his exit.

'Where go *takala?*' enquired Girish, and I said, 'He go crazy.'

If I thought I'd seen the last of Spud, however, I was wrong. Three days later as I sat in the departure lounge at Delhi airport, waiting for my flight home to Gatwick, a familiar bald head popped up.

'Hello!' said Spud, grinning. 'I bet you weren't expecting me!'

'My God!' I exclaimed. 'What are you doing here? Shouldn't you be in Thailand or something?'

'Yes,' chirped Spud, 'but unfortunately the Pink City Express from Jaipur wasn't an express after all. It got into Delhi two hours after my flight left for Bangkok. I've been holed up here in the airport hotel for the past three days, trying to get out of India.'

I was at my wits' end. This trip had been one disaster after another. Not only had Spud missed Pema on the way into India, leaving Satish to do his job for him, but he had managed to miss Pema on the way out, too, leaving me with thirty kilos of bone bracelets to lug home on my own. To top it off, he had arranged this unscheduled trip to Bangkok—and who knows where else—without consulting me. What was wrong with this guy?

Back in England, I came to understand Spud's recent erratic behaviour. I asked Tim what my 'partner' had been up to in my absence, and why I had been unable to reach him during my first two weeks in India. The answer, which Tim reluctantly told me, was alarming. Spud had fallen in with a 'bad crowd'. He had been doing not only cocaine, but ecstasy as well. He'd spent the whole fortnight whooping it up at rave parties along the M25 motorway. Spud had not done the London show; Tim had done it for him. Shock ran through me, then anger, then confusion. I had a loose cannon 'enigma' on my hands, and I didn't know what to do with him.

Everything we had worked for so long was about to go tits up.

Or was it?

Instead of following my first inclinations and confronting Spud with my discoveries, I decided to bide my time. Too much was at stake for me to rock the boat just yet.

₹

Chapter 17

Monsoon Madness

Nobody in their right mind goes to India during the monsoons. But I had no choice. It was either that or say goodbye to Spud.

In the short three week period during which Spud was gone, I unexpectedly discovered romance. I had long admired Anita, the flame-haired beauty who manned my old pitch at St Martin's, but with Spud around I had never found time to do anything about it.

Now I had, but it was not that simple.

I was crippled by a shyness that went back to my adolescence, to a time when I was a tall, thin geek with huge buck teeth, National Health glasses, and a stupid, pudding-bowl haircut. My attitude towards chatting up girls then was the same as my attitude to cold-calling on shops now: they couldn't want me, so why bother trying?

On the other hand, I had gained a lot of confidence since I'd started on the markets. Most of my customers were women, and they seemed to like me, so what was the problem? Now, with my hair swept back, my teeth fixed, and my skin perfectly tanned from India, I figured I had a chance. Besides, and I felt confident of this at least, I could make most any woman laugh.

But Anita was not just any woman. She was edgy, high-strung, and intimidating. She was also the worst saleswoman I had ever seen. If a customer took too long to buy something, she would snarl, 'Make your bloody mind up, won't you? I haven't got all day!' If they continued to dither, she would simply turn her back and mutter, quite audibly, 'Customers! I fucking *hate* customers!'

I can't explain why, but I was extremely taken with her. It's true I had always loved challenges, and she was definitely one of those, but she was also the rudest, most outrageous woman I'd ever clapped eyes on. The most cutting and suspicious, too. When I finally asked her out, she sneered at me.

'You're not my type at all,' she claimed. 'And when you ask me "out", what you really mean is "let's stay *in!*" Why don't you just bloody say so!'

She was obviously too sensitive for this world, I thought protectively. She could do with some rescuing. And so, with a persistence born of wanting something I simply couldn't have, I put aside her withering rejections and determined to try again.

The very next day, I watched, amused, as a punter took too long to decide on a silver charm bracelet. His mistake was absentmindedly tapping the table with a pencil while he deliberated. The pencil snapped moments after Anita did.

'Do you *have* to do that?' she screamed, smashing her tiny fist on the poor guy's fingers.

'What a madling!' I thought, glowing with admiration. I decided to put the 'making her laugh' idea to one side, since Anita was decidedly short on humour. Small and furious, she was spikier than a fully grown thorn bush. Only a full-scale charm offensive—something I had perfected over spending three years on a market stall—stood any chance with her. That, plus a dash of cunning and subterfuge.

She spotted me chanting round the back of the stall one day, and asked what I was doing. I seized my opportunity. 'You wouldn't be interested,' I told her.

That got her attention. 'Try me,' she said.

So I charmed myself into her small flat on the pretext of talking to her about Buddhism. But I never got round to it. Just as I opened my mouth to explain the Four Noble Truths to her, there was a power-cut. And reaching out in the gloom for my mini-Maglite torch, I found something *far* more interesting – one of her generously-sized breasts. 'Whoops!' I said innocently. 'I thought that was the light switch!' And in the awkward silence that followed, as the heat unexpectedly rose between us, Anita reached down and grabbed my crotch.

I would later quote this experience as one of the most conspicuous benefits of my entire Buddhist practice.

*

What distinguished Anita from all my previous girlfriends was her sheer presence. Though only five foot tall on tippy-toes, she oozed charisma. Heads turned wherever she went. Her pretty, doll-like face was framed by a mass of bright-orange curls, and she had an hourglass figure most women would have killed for. A fireball of fierce energy and quick intelligence, Anita reminded me of only one other person, and that was Spud. Except she was far more attractive.

From the very start, I was in love.

Anita was an actress. She had studied at RADA, the prestigious London drama school, and had just split up with her soon-to-be-famous boyfriend Gary Oldman. Anita would have liked to be famous, too, but her diminutive frame (along with her temperament) made her unsuitable for most parts. Moreover, she was convinced that she was 'too good' for small roles. They were beneath her, she said – she would only consider 'major Shakespeare like Lady Macbeth'. Her agent, an owlish figure named Bunny, was in constant despair. So far he had only managed to get Anita fleeting cameos as big-bosomed barmaids in soaps like *Eastenders.* It was this lack of productivity, more than anything, that prompted Anita to leave Gary. He had just had his first big movie break, playing Sid Vicious in the punk film *Sid and Nancy*, and she couldn't handle the competition. It made her even more insecure than she was already.

Anita's main insecurity concerned her weight. She had been fat as a child and was still fat inside her own mind. That first night together, after we had collided in the dark, she told me, 'You can make love to me, but leave the lights off. I don't want you to see how fat I am.'

I had tried to persuade her otherwise, but she had uncharacteristically burst into tears, and I'd had to hold her for hours until she calmed down. I was disappointed to discover that the lovemaking, when it finally happened, was good for me but not for her.

'I'm sorry,' she sniffed defensively, 'but I've got trust issues. My father left when I was very young, and I've never found a man I can truly relax with.'

'I can be that man,' I reassured her. 'I'll do everything in my power to make you happy.'

With that I took her off the market stall, paid her rent and all her expenses, and generally removed every trace of stress from her life.

'You're worth it,' I said softly, pulling her close. 'You're warm and funny and cuddly and cute. You're everything I need.'

The next day, very cautiously, she held my hand in public.

I met her ex, Gary, just once, at Camden Market, and found him surprisingly candid. 'She's a real head case,' he said, 'but never boring.' He then handed me the twin cats he had reared with her, Thomas and Rhetty. 'The same goes for these two,' he said.

The cats moved in with me the same day that Anita did, and suddenly, from being a lone wolf banging about in a huge house full of Indian clothing, I found myself part of a rowdy rat-pack. Tom and Rhetty may have been brother and sister, but it didn't stop them fighting all the time, and it was the same with me and Anita. As Gary had intimated, Anita was a total diva and super-sensitive to criticism. She also had a formidable temper. In the first week of our relationship, I had a dustbin, two ashtrays and a bag of cat litter thrown at me. And I was lucky.

*

When Spud returned from his sojourn of Southeast Asia, I had a new roommate in Anita, and Spud found himself cut adrift. He still wanted all my time and attention, but he couldn't get it. Anita demanded a whole lot of both.

Anita reserved her special scorn for Spud. Her first words to him, as he tried to invade the house one morning, were, 'What the fuck do *you* want?' She then slammed the door in his face and returned to her karaoke tapes while he vainly tapped at the window.

It was even worse when I returned and put the two of them together. At one point Anita caught Spud helplessly gazing down her fulsome cleavage and demanded, 'What are you looking at, you walking *cock?*'

Sadly, that was almost true, for Spud's bald head turned quite purple with lust and was wobbling phallically as he strove to contain it. Totally lost for words and embarrassed beyond belief, he charged out of the house and unleashed his rage on the helpless van parked outside. He emptied all its contents into the road, stomped on them, then rammed the vehicle into a tree.

'Is he always like that?' asked Anita, intrigued.

'No,' I replied. 'Maybe you just bring out the best in him.' Then I headed outside to have a chat with Spud. 'Have you quite finished?' I enquired with a smile.

'No, I fucking haven't!' raged Spud. 'Who *is* that mad bitch?'

'That's Nita,' I informed him. 'You gave her my job at St Martin's, remember? And you're going to have to put up with her, because she's just moved in. And so have her two cats.'

Spud's head went purple again, but this time with rage. 'Next you'll be telling me she's a vegetarian astrologer!' he ranted. 'Get rid of her! We can't run a business with a woman in our warehouse!'

'You tell her!' I said. 'You're the one she caught staring at her tits!'

I was secretly having fun. It was the first time I had seen Spud, so very good at scaring other people, scared himself. I knew Spud wasn't going back in that house. Nobody who had experienced the dark side of Anita ever wanted seconds. It had been like watching a Pit-bull and a Doberman going head to head, that first exchange of my two 'partners', and I couldn't wait for it to happen again.

That night at around 2am, I stopped having fun. Anita, ever sensitive to noise, shot up in bed. 'I heard the door,' she whispered urgently. 'There's a burglar downstairs!'

I didn't think twice. While Anita bolted for the bathroom, scooping up two cats as she went, I grabbed my trusty air-pistol from under the bed, ran stark naked to the top of the stairs and—with no spectacles to help me—fired blindly down. I obviously hit something, because I heard a pained squawk before the intruder fled the house.

The next morning, Spud appeared, nursing a large bruise on his neck. 'I only came to borrow your van keys,' he snarled. 'You didn't have to fucking *shoot* me!'

'You could have been anybody!' I protested. 'And besides, what's wrong with your van?'

Spud sniffed and glared blackly at me. 'My van is inoperative owing to "action of tree,"' he said. 'Besides, "anybody" wouldn't have had your front door key, would they?'

There was no point continuing the discussion. Both of us knew Anita was the catalyst for both events: Spud crashing his van and Spud being shot as an intruder. And if she had caused such chaos in just one day, what was she capable of next? As Spud retired to lick his wounds, I sat Anita down and patiently explained to her that I had a business to run, and that since Spud was a necessary part of that business, he had to be tolerated.

'He's a rude, insolent little pervert,' sniffed Anita. 'I don't like him.'

I shrugged. 'You don't have to like him,' I persisted. 'Just let him in occasionally to restock his van, and stay out of his way.'

'Fair enough,' said Anita. 'But you told me I was moving into a house, not a *warehouse*, and staying out of his way isn't possible. He'll be in and out of here on a daily basis, putting up shelving, restocking your markets, and generally turning this place into an Indian *godown.*' She shook her head. 'I've been watching you two for a while, you know. That little git thinks he owns you. But as far as I can see, it's the other way round. He relies on you for just about everything: money, friends, contacts in India, this huge stock-palace, even the goodwill of your customers. No wonder he controls your every move. Without you, he'd be nothing!'

I had never before looked at things that way. Up until now I had considered myself to be Spud's equal in every respect. But then I remembered half-forgotten events, like the time Spud had made me erect scaffolding despite my badly twisted ankle, or the time he dragged me off my sickbed with the cynical remark: 'You can't pull a sickie on me now. There's work to do!'

Was Spud really that much of a control freak that he felt the need to regularly put me down, to show me who was boss? If Anita was right in her assessment, Spud was so afraid he might become a 'jilted lover' and be left behind, that he was seizing control wherever he could find it. It struck me now, for instance, that Spud had sole say on the company finances. He, and only he decided who got paid and how much. I knew there was a joint chequebook out there somewhere, but I hadn't seen it, let alone been allowed to sign it.

The thing that worried me the most was how Spud had taken over the buying end of things, when he obviously had no talent for it. Spud's solo tour of the Orient had been a disaster. After leaving me stranded in Jaipur, he had spent six days in Bangkok, of which at least four had been spent blowing up condoms in bars and getting free drinks for putting them on his bald head. When he had arrived in Vietnam, he'd found it 'closed' for Chinese New Year. Finally he had gone to Bali and spent a whole week chasing tailors, trying unsuccessfully to get them to make batik clothing for him. To top it all, every gram of silver he had bought in his travels had been impounded when he'd flown into London three days ago.

Anita's comments hit home. For the first time, I realised how ineffective Spud was on his own, and how close I had come to allowing him to completely take over my life. I also realised that if Spud had thus far been my protection against the likes of the Petrovs, Anita was now my only protection against Spud.

₹

Chapter 18

Spud vs Nita

In truth, I didn't need protection. I needed the freedom to consider a very difficult choice. Spud and Anita, one of them had to go. And since neither was willing to be number two on someone's list of priorities, I had to decide soon. On impulse, I booked myself a flight to India during the hottest, wettest, most uncomfortable time of year.

'You're going *where?*' Spud demanded. 'You've only been back a month!' Spud had no grounds on which to complain. He had, after all, only just returned from his own unauthorised holiday.

But Anita was incensed. 'You're doing *what*?' she shrieked. 'We've only had three weeks together! Don't expect me to be here when you get back,' she warned. 'I'm fed up with being messed around by men!'

The hardest thing I had ever had to do was leave Nita on such short notice. But the moment I boarded the plane I felt an immense wave of relief. 'No more worries for a while,' I thought. 'Time and space to consider my options.'

Then I touched down in Delhi airport and stepped into a smouldering, suffocating cauldron of heat. I was back in the capital at the height of summer, sweating through 44 degrees in the shade with not a hint of a breeze.

To make matters worse, I was on holiday, and I hated holidays. I was too restless a soul to sit in a beach chair. With ten days to kill before I could return to the UK, and with boredom already setting in, I needed a plan.

So I did a bit of chanting and remembered an old plan I had been putting off for years. In a rare mood of spontaneity, I decided to take a twenty hour taxi ride down to Bhuj in search of old embroidery. Bhuj was the capital of Kutch state, and it was the last place likely to have the antique zari bedspreads which sold so well in the UK.

A day or so later I stood at the travel desk of the Pushkar Palace, haggling with the manager, Deepak, over taxi hire. It was incredibly cheap by western standards—only £2 an hour—but since I would be travelling long distances each day, I was being charged a lot more for extra diesel.

'I'll pay you a flat daily rate of 1000 rupees,' I declared at last. 'Subject, that is, to a 200 rupee penalty for every problem I have with your taxi or its driver!'

When Deepak enquired what constituted a problem, I reeled off the following list for him:

1. Uninvited drunken passengers

2. Uninvited pets or animals

3. Bald tyres and even balder spare tyres

4. Loud blaring Hindi music on warped car-stereo systems

5. Non-English-speaking drivers with no sense of direction

6. Unlicensed taxis making long detours to avoid policemen

7. Taxis turning up an hour early, an hour late, or not at all

8. Unsolicited stops in Ajmer while driver's wife has a baby

Deepak regarded me quizzically, but I was having no argument. I spoke from experience.

The following morning I set off for Bhuj, already 1000 rupees in credit. The car was late, it had three bald tyres, and a cat had taken up lodgings on my seat. Furthermore, not only had my driver never been to Bhuj, he didn't even know where it was. I told Deepak all this, and he shrugged.

'I can do nothing,' he said.

My driver was named Pintoo, and, like most rural taxi drivers, he had his own agenda. The first thing he did was go to a gas station and fill up, which was something he should have done beforehand. The second thing he did was take a ten kilometre detour to his family house to pick up a spare shirt. We finally left Ajmer around noon, with me studying a roadmap and an anxious Pintoo asking, 'Which way?' every five minutes.

As darkness fell, Pintoo switched on his headlamps – only to find they didn't work. As I began sellotaping the full-beam indicator to the steering wheel, hoping to produce enough light to proceed, Pintoo squatted at my side and began happily filling me in on local temples. He wanted to go do *darshan* at one of them and when I said no, he got quite sulky. I think he wanted to apologise to dairy-god Krishna for the cow he had nudged into a ditch earlier.

We plunged on into the night, and I let my mind wander. I found myself replaying a conversation I'd had a few nights before with Gordhan back in Jaipur. He had driven me to an air-conditioned restaurant, force-fed me a vegetarian *thali*, and said, 'You have big tension in your head, Frankie. What is problem?'

'I don't know what to do,' I'd confided. 'I have new girlfriend, Anita, and she is enemy of Spud. One person must go, but who should it be?'

Gordhan's response had been typically Indian. 'No life without wife,' he'd declared with authority. 'But girlfriend is not wife. And Spud is money-maker, lucky for you. My advice is keep the Spud and lose the Nita!'

I wasn't convinced. 'Really? But I love her. And it's been four years of backbreaking hard work since I've had time to love anyone. Also, she counts on me for just about everything: food, clothing, money, and lodgings. Why should she go?'

'Then you are free ox!' Gordhan stated pragmatically. 'No expensive cow!'

I had to give him that. Anita certainly was working out to be expensive. The Oberoi hotel in Delhi now had my record phone bill stuck to its reception wall. It amounted to £293, which related to a three-hour call I'd made to Anita trying to persuade her not to leave me just yet.

'What are you *doing* out there?' she'd shouted in the end. 'If you don't come back right now, I'm off!'

'Off where?' I'd asked cautiously. 'You've got no job, no money, and nowhere to live.'

'Don't remind me!' she snarled. 'I think it's about time I took responsibility for my own life, and I can't do that when I'm living on your charity!'

'It's not charity,' I told her. 'I want to look after you!'

'Yeah, right,' she concluded. 'You're just like my dad. First you spoil me rotten, then you up and leave!'

Two hours down the line from Ahmedabad, the capital of Gujarat, Pintoo announced he had a 'big stomach problem.' I asked if it was something he had eaten, but he said no. He blamed the bottle of mineral water I had given him in Pushkar. I told him it had been thoroughly filtered and purified, but Pintoo was insistent.

'No more tourist bottle!' he moaned. 'I like tap water. It is good for tummy!'

He might have had a point. Maybe pure bottled water had the same effect on Indians that local tap water had on foreigners. If so, I would soon be giving away my last toilet roll.

Too tired by now to read any more maps, I handed them forward to Pintoo, then fell, exhausted, into a long, deep sleep on the back seat.

This was not one of my better ideas.

I awoke six hours later to discover I was not in Bhuj. In fact, I was not even in the right state. Pintoo had merrily plunged us deep into the heart of Gujarat, not the Rann of Kutch. He was 300 kilometres off course.

'Nice sleep?' he enquired with a smile, and I felt like slapping him.

'Why you make like this?' I snapped. Pintoo handed me back my map and I noticed the entire state of Kutch had been erased by the remains of his thali dinner.

We eventually rolled up at the five star Gir Lodge in Sasan Gir. The lodge had been built recently to accommodate the busloads of rich Indians wanting to see the Asiatic lion roaming his last natural refuge on earth.

All I wanted to see was a hot bath and a soft bed.

I was relieved that I had only paid half the trip upfront. The other half, I phoned Deepak to say, was now forfeit. Pintoo's total lack of direction had added a whole day to my tour, and I was paying £70 for a luxury hotel in which I didn't even want to stay. Deepak's response, when it came, was curiously satisfying. There was a strangled cry at the other end of the phone. 'No pay? *Why* no pay?'

I didn't bother answering.

The next morning, much refreshed, I went down for breakfast. I took a seat, then slowly became aware that if I thought the waiters in Pushkar were bad, I hadn't seen anything yet. The Gir Lodge was the only five star property for hundreds of miles. And it took me thirty minutes to get a three-minute egg out of them.

To be fair, the hotel had only just opened, and it hadn't had time to properly train its staff. The waiter I got had a month before been herding goats in some nearby village. And the reason he took so long with the three-minute egg was that he didn't know how to turn the gas on. When he eventually drifted back to ask for help, I took a long hard look at him and decided he was in the wrong job. He should have stuck to goats. His smart khaki uniform sat uneasily on him, and his feet squirmed inside his new patent plastic shoes. His hair had obviously been plastered down early that morning, and it was beginning to fly out of shape. But it was his eyes that really told the story. They were flitting all over the place, like a jackrabbit caught in a trap.

'Butter?' he intoned forlornly, and when I said no, he nearly burst into tears.

There was nothing to be done, I decided, but sit back and wait. The cook had arrived, and I felt reasonably sure that if anybody could make a three-minute egg, it would be him. Sure enough, eight minutes later, the egg appeared. Actually, there were two of them. They sat small and lonely in a soup bowl the size of an army tureen. As I chased them round the bowl with a tiny teaspoon, my tousled waiter reappeared.

'Drink?' he offered hesitantly.

'Beer?' I replied hopefully.

'Yus!' said the waiter and came back with a lemon soda.

'Is this man deaf?' I asked a passing receptionist.

'No,' came the answer. 'He is just not thinking very much.'

An hour later we were back on the road. And what a long, long road it was. Even haunting Pintoo with my new roadmap and shouting repeated directions over his shoulder, we didn't roll into Bhuj until midnight. Too late to get any food, and too late to get even the most basic of lodgings, I drank the last of my Black Panther rum and scrunched up on the back seat of the taxi, silently cursing Deepak as I slid into oblivion.

The trip to Bhuj was, ironically, far more exciting than actually getting there. Upon waking, I made a quick reconnaissance of the town and came to one conclusion: I had just driven two days for absolutely nothing. A German buyer had just bought every scrap of old embroidery for miles around, and there was nothing left but tat.

But I liked Bhuj. It was, even at cursory inspection, the most atmospheric town to which I'd ever been, full of mediaeval charm and character. I would have liked to stay longer, but Pintoo had other ideas. He wasn't feeling well, he said, and he wanted to go home. So we loaded up with more toilet rolls and sellotape (for the head beam) and set off back to Pushkar.

Along the way my passenger window suddenly detached itself from its moorings and fell into the road. This happened, ironically, just as Pintoo was exalting his Ambassador taxi as being 'positively the finest car in all the world.' It took him ten minutes to retrieve the missing glass, then he couldn't get back in the car again because the driver's door was jammed.

I didn't hear any more about the Ambassador for the rest of

the ride.

We limped into Pushkar after dark, my head stuck in Pintoo's lap as I tried to re-tape the erratic head beam, and Pintoo yelling '*Bastard* car!' out the window at startled locals. This phrase, which he mimicked with uncanny accuracy, was the only new English he had learned throughout his time with me.

I was finished. Totally exhausted. I collapsed onto my bed at the Palace Hotel and fell into a long, dreamless sleep.

Back in Jaipur the next day, I braced myself and phoned up Spud in England – something I had been putting off ever since our fracas over Anita. This call took 50 minutes and cost an alarming £160. It only cost that much because I caught Spud at his stubborn, most obnoxious worst. All I wanted to know was whether he had put my delivery van in for service yet, since it was due for an inspection. There was a long pause at the other end of the telephone, then Spud asked, 'Do you know what a full service *involves?*'

I told him I didn't care what it involved, I just needed one.

There was an even longer pause before Spud tried again. 'You don't *know* what a full service involves, do you?'

Sure enough, when I eventually got back to London, I found my van exactly where I'd left it. When I took it to the garage and had it serviced myself, the bill came to a lot less than it had cost to phone Spud from India and not get it done at all. I reckoned he had not got over his humiliation at the hands of Anita, so he hadn't dared face the diminutive harpy again to ask for the van keys.

On my last night in Jaipur, Girish drove me—with manic carelessness—to see a film entitled *Prodigal Son*. He said he wanted to take my mind off things. Gordhan had already described the movie to me as being 'half good and half bad.'

When asked which half was good and which half was bad, he had replied, 'The first half is half good and half bad, and the second half is half good and half bad.' This was a problem, since Hindi films were so long that I could usually only endure the first half. But I didn't want to miss the half-good bit of the second half, so I reconciled myself to seeing the whole film. All five hours of it.

In the end, neither half had much to recommend it except that the villain couldn't have been more villainous if he tried. Not only was he fat, greasy, and aggressive, but he didn't go anywhere without a shotgun. He also carried around three other props: a cigarette drooping off his bottom lip, a pair of reflecting Raybans, and a snivelling lackey with bad teeth. What distinguished him from every other screen villain I had seen before was his appalling taste in clothes. His jackets were particularly nasty, progressing from garish Laura Ashley prints to nerve-jangling colour-clash geometric designs. I was fairly sure it was his dress sense, rather than any personal shortcomings, that finally drove the flute-playing hero to shove him off a cliff.

On leaving the cinema, I asked Girish whether he had enjoyed the film. He shook his head doubtfully. 'This one not last two weeks.'

*

My time in India was now up, and it was crunch time. I could no longer avoid Spud or Anita. I had to go home and make that fateful decision between the two of them.

But in my absence, the decision had already been made. After spending ten long hours in a plane, every minute full of agonising and soul-searching, I stepped back into my house in

Peckham and found three things: an empty wardrobe, a pair of hungry cats, and a 'Dear John' letter from Anita. Yes, she had decided to leave me. Not for the obvious reason – Spud – but because 'I think I'm happier by myself. I just don't have the talent for being half a couple.' She wanted to be alone to resume her acting career, she wrote, and would I look after her pussies? The cats were no problem – I had come to love them dearly – but her abrupt departure most certainly was.

'My only regret is that I might have hurt you,' concluded the letter. 'If I have, I'm truly sorry. But I think you are also a fairly self-contained type of person. Neither of us will be lonely, I'm sure of that.'

I was not so sure. In our short time together, Anita had become a light in my life, a sweet but fragile companion, and I was really going to miss her.

The only person happy with the news was Spud. He left me alone for a couple of days, just so as not to appear too happy, then he turned up with the following fax from Gordhan.

> _I hope this finds you in a healthy and cheerful_
> _mood after your business tour. Also, I wish this_
> _day to be as happy and gay as a lily in May. We_
> _shall ship your jackets at our earliest possible!_

Spud and I laughed out loud, and in our laughter we were reconciled.

₹

Chapter 19

Mister Order Cancel Man

It was January 1995, and Spud had been in India for two weeks. His idea had been to fly ahead and 'lay some groundwork' so that when I arrived all our goods would be under production. Something told me it wouldn't work out that way, but I had decided – a year or so down the line – to give Spud one last chance at buying. After all Spud had done for me, rescuing me from a lonely market stall and making me one of the biggest wholesalers in the UK, I figured he deserved that much.

I had just settled into the Oberoi in Delhi and was watching a 'best-dressed cow in Madras' competition on TV, when Spud burst into my room.

'It's all done, mate!' he proclaimed. 'You've only got about two hours' work in Pushkar, then you can have a holiday!'

He flung a load of orders and a bundle of mixed currency at me, and ran off to catch his plane back to England.

The first rumblings I had that Spud's attempt at solo buying in India had gone awry came three days later, when I arrived in Jaipur. Gordhan wasn't happy with Spud, who had accused him of 'running a circus, with Sharma and Rakesh as the chief clowns.' The reason for his declaration was because Spud had ordered 2000 metres of block-print material to be made, and after two weeks Sharma and Rakesh had produced just twenty-four metres—all of it in the wrong print.

'So much for "only two hours' work and then you can have a holiday!"' I sighed to myself. It would take me two hours just to calm Gordhan down, then to cancel Spud's order.

The trend continued in Pushkar, where Spud had dropped several more bombshells. I spent my first day there cancelling orders. The only order I didn't cancel, even though I wanted to, was for 2000 Dennis the Menace T-shirts from Mendu. These had been made already, and Spud had ordered them in just one size: his own.

'How many people you know in size like Spud?' I asked.

Mendu replied, 'Not one possible!'

I had no choice but to cancel Spud's orders. Spud hadn't left clear instructions, so the clothes hadn't been made well. The worst offender by far was the short dungarees he'd dreamt up in some Delhi toilet. Satish had attempted a sample, but when he'd tried it on some hippy chick in the market, it looked like a pair of tie-dye incontinence pants. By the end of the day, I had cancelled all evidence of Spud's 'buying' trip and resigned myself to starting again from scratch.

But the nightmare was not yet over. As I flicked through the last of Spud's orders, I was horrified to spot the name of Isaak Mohammed. For some indefinable reason, Spud had resumed negotiations with the worst tailor in town. He had also given him an order for five hundred tie-and-dye smocks.

I charged down to Isaak's shop to see how this particular order was progressing. Turns out it wasn't progressing at all, because Isaak wasn't there.

'He's in hiding,' Susie called down.

I was surprised to hear her voice. Evidently she had

claimed the rooftop hovel over Isaak's quarters and had made it her new home. I climbed the stairs to see her.

'In hiding from what?' I asked.

'From you. He heard you were coming into town, and he shut his shop.'

I slumped. 'Okay,' I said. 'What's wrong?'

'Oh, you haven't heard. Well, you'd better sit down.' Susie balanced baby Om Prakash with one arm and handed me a cup of cardamom tea with the other.

'It's Spud, isn't it?'

She grinned. 'How did you guess?'

I sighed, resigned. How could I not?

'You remember how cross he was last trip, when Isaak didn't make your goods on time?' she asked.

Yes, I certainly did remember that. We had got so fed up with waiting for Isaak that we had given him a new name: Mister Shanti, or Mister Ultra-Slow. He had been so wazzed out on bhang lassis it had taken him three days to cut one piece of material in half.

'Well, Spud wanted someone to make him five hundred chiffon smocks, and nobody but Isaak would do it. They were … ahem … so transparent that even I wouldn't try one on. And you know I'm open to pretty much anything.'

'So?'

'So he asked Isaak to make a sample, and Isaak forgot to make it. Spud found him downstairs, tranced out on another bhang lassi. This time Spud grabbed hold of Isaak, marched him out to the desert, and began force feeding him mutton curry.'

I stared, and she nodded. 'Everyone in town is talking about it.'

It took a moment before I could find words. 'He did *what?*'

135

'It gets worse. This happened during the holy feast of Ramadan, when Isaak was supposed to be fasting. I don't know what's happened to Spud, Frank. Someone said he's on drugs. Whatever it was, he was well on his way to inviting an international fatwa!'

Susie went off to welcome Raju back from work, leaving me to sit back and think. For some reason I recognised this little scenario of Spud's ... now where was it? It wasn't Tarantino's *Reservoir Dogs*, though I could well imagine Spud dancing around the annoyingly sleepy little Muslim with a lit match and a can of petrol. And no, it wasn't any number of hostage movies Spud and I had watched together on Indian video buses.

At last, light dawned. It had in fact been a conversation with Girish on our last trip in Jaipur, to which both of us had been privy. In that conversation we learnt that nobody stole from the Jaipur Agarwals and got away with it. Earlier that day a cleaner had stolen £1000 from Gordhan's house, along with a solid gold necklace. A few hours later, Girish caught him, but he didn't take him to the police station. Oh no. Instead, he drove him to an empty building and stripped the man naked. He stood on the wretch's feet with hobnail boots, warmed up a pair of sugar tongs to white heat, then branded him about the body until he returned the loot. Then—and this could only happen in India—he gave the thief five hundred rupees to go away and never come back.

'Did Spud offer Isaak money, by any chance?' I asked on Susie's return.

'How did you know?' she said, surprised. 'Yes, he waited until Isaak's master tailor miraculously came up with a sample. It only took him twenty minutes! Then he gave Isaak five hundred rupees to go away and never talk to him again.'

'But that doesn't apply to me. Why is Isaak hiding from me?'

'*Everyone's* hiding from you! Haven't you noticed? They all think Spud is crazy, and if they get stuff wrong, you're going to tell him and he's going to come back and torture them!'

That explained a lot. Cancelling Spud's orders had been easy. Placing new ones was proving to be impossible. The favourite excuse I'd been getting was that it was the marriage season, and all the tailors were on holiday. The best excuse by far came from Mendu who, when I asked him to make five hundred block-print shirts, said, 'So sorry. Tailor is dead.'

When I asked where his other six tailors were, and why they were not working, he replied, 'Oh, they go to funeral.'

Inevitably, the only person I could find to work for me was Satish Agarwal. I found the man squashed deep inside his hole-in-the-wall grotto like a fat spider awaiting his prey. I tried to lure him out, but he wasn't having it. He was hiding, very sensibly, from the intense heat.

'Come inside,' he crooned. 'Enjoy ice cold mango Frooti drink!'

'Okay,' I said, 'but please, no business. First we talk friendship.'

'Friendship is good,' muttered Satish. 'We can talk money after. Why not?'

Satish, I knew already, was an Agarwal, just like Gordhan in Jaipur. It was his self-proclaimed 'duty' to make money. What I did not know, and what served to explain Satish's apparent greed, was that the Agarwals were a business caste. The more money he made, the more people looked up to them. I couldn't understand this at all. In my country, I told Satish, flaunting one's wealth was regarded as bad taste. Only people like Spud actually *enjoyed* flaunting it—carrying a grand around in his pockets, for example, just for show. But Satish wasn't showy. As the eldest brother of three, he explained, he had a large extended family to support. He didn't make money for its own sake. He made it for all of them.

Satish must have been a striking man in his youth, I thought. Even now, aged thirty-six, he looked exactly like Omar Sharif. He had the same moist-brown eyes, the same aquiline nose, the same seductive smile. Even the same moustache and dimpled chin. The only thing that wasn't the same was the three stones of excess weight he carried. He'd lost it once and tourists started asking for his autograph.

Everyone has their Achilles heel, however. In Satish's case it was his lazy left eye. The right one gleamed with warm sincerity and bonhomie. It said, 'I am your friend and servant. You can trust me with your life.' The left one, by contrast, was a narrow slit with a restless ball which wandered to and fro instead of looking straight ahead. It said, 'I am a devious bastard who is about to cheat you. I hope you don't notice.' Satish's left eye was unfortunate, because it put off every other wholesaler from dealing with him. Nick found him 'creepy' and George, who had a thing about evil eyes anyway, wrote him off as an 'asswipe.'

Once you got past the eye, however, Satish was about the friendliest person imaginable. He was so friendly that he actually scared people away. I had to sit him down one day and encourage him to relax.

'You have too much mental tension,' I told him. 'Let customer come to you, not you to them!'

Satish took my advice to heart, and not long after, he became the teacher and I his willing disciple. He stood in the entrance of his shop in the Pushkar market, arms akimbo, and flashed his teeth at passing lady tourists. If any of them came close enough, he gave them a present. A shawl, perhaps, or a scarf. Satish had learned since he was old enough to rub two rupees together that his profit rose in direct proportion to the number of presents he gave his customers. And his psychology, which I quickly adopted, was spot-on. Once he had hooked them with a present, they felt duty-bound to buy something from him. First they bought something cheap, just to return the favour. Then, when he gave them another present, they bought something more expensive. And so it continued until they had one armful of presents which had cost them nothing, and another armful of purchases which had probably cost them double what they would've paid anywhere else. So Satish ended up with lots of profit, they held lots of presents, and everybody was happy.

Over one more frozen Frooti, I asked Satish how he had first come to Pushkar.

'That is a long story, Frankie!' he said, chucking a friendly arm around me. 'How much time you have?'

I indicated the empty street. All the shops were closed for siesta. 'A lot.'

So he settled in to tell his tale. I learnt that one winter, when Satish was ten, his father had travelled to Pushkar for the Camel Fair. Once there, he'd decided to open a blanket shop. Hordes of pilgrims had flooded in for the fair, all of them wanting something on which to sit during the day, and something to wrap around themselves when the desert grew cold at night. Woollen blankets were very much in demand. His family already had a successful jewellery business to the north, in Mathura, but Satish's dad had been having problems with his partner and wanted to try something new. So he uprooted the whole family and brought them 360 kilometres west to Pushkar. It was a shrewd move, but not without complications. The main complication was that they were not welcome. The young Satish liked Pushkar, but the Pushkar people didn't like him. He was an outsider, a migrant pariah who was certain to take food out of their mouths by setting up a competing business. They wouldn't even walk in his shadow.

'I don't like the local people situation,' confided Satish. 'Too much blub-blub-blub, and no friendship-making. I like business for customer relation, not for money only!'

Satish left school at age fourteen to help his father with the cloth business. But two years later his father died, leaving Satish in charge of the whole family. He had two younger brothers, Sanjay and Dinesh, but they had been too young to work. It had been up to him to keep things going.

'Now my name in Pushkar is very popular,' said Satish. 'But first five years is hard. I work alone and nobody want to be my friend.'

Satish then told me of his two brothers, who were also Agarwal. They weren't as fat as he was, he joked, because they worked more and had less money. In fact, because they were younger and had fewer responsibilities, the Agarwal rules meant they couldn't actually make money for themselves at all. They could only help him make money, and this they were pleased to do. The reason they were so happy to serve him was because Satish would soon choose their wives, and the richer they helped Satish become, the more well-born and attractive these wives would be. In the meantime, all the money they made for Satish went into the family pot and secured all their futures.

The youngest brother, Sanjay, grinned a lot. He was the most handsome of the three, and he knew it. He had the dark swarthy features of a Rajput chieftain, and the slim, dangerous grace of a panther on the prowl. Western ladies swooned over him, and he usually courted two or three at the same time. They loved his shock of shiny black hair and his doe-like eyes. They particularly liked his roguish grin, which, if he could have bottled it, would have made him a fortune. Satish encouraged Sanjay's grin because it sold a whole lot of clothing and made him a fortune. Unknown to Sanjay—and here I was sworn to strict secrecy—Satish had no intention of marrying him off for a long time. It wouldn't be good for business.

Dinesh, the middle brother, was the holy one, since he was a bit simple, and therefore close to God. Dinesh spent half his day doing *puja* (prayers) for the family and the other half working out. Just as Satish collected money and Sanjay foreign girlfriends, Dinesh collected muscles – and, of course, good karma for the Agarwals.

Dinesh made me nervous. Dinesh made *everyone* nervous. Not just because he was a large, frisky puppy-dog, but because he was dangerously affectionate. The first time I met Dinesh I had been in the shop, checking jackets. Dinesh had sprung up out of nowhere to pump my hand and comment on my progress.

'I know your *mind!*' he exclaimed, beaming happily. 'I know what you are *thinking!*'

But he had caught me on a bad day, and I snapped back, 'Okay, if you know my mind so well, I'll go home and *you* can check these jackets!'

Dinesh paused a moment, trying to decide if I were serious or not. Then he leapt over to give me such a crushing bear hug my lungs nearly imploded. 'Ha, ha, *ha!*' he boomed. 'You are good joking man. That is *good!*'

₹

Chapter 20

Full Moon Camel Trek

I left Satish with an order for four hundred wool jackets then walked back up the market. Up a little way, George was taking part in a heated debate with Mendu about the price of cotton dresses. As the volume of their shouting grew, Mendu's face twisted into a grotesque leer, and he played his ace card.

'Where is my *watch?*' he screamed.

George, who had quite forgot he'd promised Mendu a watch from Pittsburgh, was forced to back down and accept the hiked prices.

'Man,' George said to me afterwards, 'that dude plays hardball!'

'Well, what do you expect?' I asked, laughing. 'You taught him the game!'

George smiled grimly, then handed me a fax he had received from Mendu in America.

> *Being well and in healthy possessions, I wish to*
> *the god for your sounding position. Very earlier, I*
> *have sent your material what you ordered. But*
> *why have you not cleared that material? If you*
> *have any problem, please inform me because the*

goods are in airline and have to be damaging. I
await your untimely information.

'What do you make of that?' he asked, looking entirely
bewildered. 'I showed it to Mendu, who wrote it, and he didn't
understand it either!'

Distracted by a passing beggar child, George then delved
into his pockets and came up with what he termed 'a
mysterious potpourri of international currency.' When he
opened his hand I saw nickels, roubles, dimes, dinars, shekels,
pence, and pfennigs, all collected down umpteen years of
travel. He gave the child a choice.

'You can have all this change,' he told her, 'or a pack of
chewing gum.'

The kid took the gum.

'That made her day,' I said.

'Yeah, well,' sniffed George. 'You can be poor in India and
still be happy, you know. Even on a stick of gum. You gotta
think about that.'

Later on, we found ourselves sitting among a Druidic circle
of new age travellers at the Sunset Cafe, listening to some
long-haired dude sing forty-two verses of 'American Pie.' He
was really getting into it, almost sobbing with emotion. The
only thing which averted his total collapse into hysteria was
the moment when George grabbed his ukulele and launched
into his favourite song: 'All I want is one more *fuck!*' The
magic circle instantly disintegrated.

'Well, that went well,' I commented. 'Who were those
guys, anyway?'

'Freaks, man,' George said with a shrug. 'Pushkar's full of
kids who missed the '60s and want to go back there. They
smoke dope, they wear tie-dye, and they wobble their heads to

eastern mantras or to Bob Marley. They're kinda sad, you know?'

'No, I don't know,' I replied. 'I would've loved to have been a hippy in India twenty years ago, hanging out on beaches in Goa, drifting north to Manali in the hot months, then hanging out again in Pushkar in the spring and living on bananas and brown rice.'

'You, as a hippy?' snorted George. 'I don't *think* so, man!'

'Why not?'

'Well, for one thing, you like eggs and chips and fried breakfasts. No brown rice for you! For another, you don't look the part. You're a geek, Frank.'

'A geek?'

'Yeah, an endearing, absent-minded college kind of a dude. Be grateful. A geek's better than an asshole and a whole lot better than an asswipe!'

I hesitated, then nodded vaguely. 'Thank you,' I said. 'I think.'

A few days later, Tim, my young UK helper, turned up in Pushkar. His eyed me cautiously. 'Be gentle with me,' he pleaded. 'I've just spent two weeks with Spud, putting on another show. I'm shot to pieces.'

Tim was a tall, lanky redhead with a ponytail and a wide, freckly smile. Of all the staff Spud had hired down the years, he was the only one who had any knowledge of India. That was why he was here to help me out. He was also the only one I trusted, and who shared my unease over Spud's deteriorating state of mind. But when I cautiously asked how things were going back home, all Tim said was, 'You don't want to know.'

That told me two things. First off, things weren't going well. Secondly, Tim was afraid of losing his job by saying why.

With the Full Moon approaching, everyone—Ram and Eri, Susie and Raju, George, Tim, and I—congregated for the annual camel trek. Even Nick and Anna were present, having just dashed up from Madras on a night train. The trek was insane: ten people dancing around a bonfire in the middle of the desert, singing Rajasthani folk songs for which they never quite learnt the words. The only people not dancing were Guy and Trudi, a Belgian couple who had no sense of humour at all. The dancing continued around the bathing ghats overlooking Pushkar lake, with everyone wearing pointy hats and trying to scare each other with their respective shadows. After three or four bhang lassis apiece, that wasn't difficult.

*

On the way home, Susie taught me the Hindi word for duck. 'It's *butak*,' she said, grinning. 'And I only know because Raju ran up to me in the street today, shouting, *"Jyoti!* Come quick! There are forty *buttocks* in the lake!'

But Susie was a little preoccupied with an important issue. For a while now, she and Raju had wanted to ensure they could legally get Raju and the children into England. They had got 'married' five times in the hopes that one of the various Hindi ceremonies they used might be considered "legal" enough to satisfy the British Immigration Service. But she still had not obtained a UK work visa for Raju, and their 'marriage' still wasn't recognised in England. She was at her wits' end.

'Don't tell anyone,' she confided to me, 'but there's another baby on the way.'

Back in the market the next day, I tried to collect Spud's tie-and-dye smocks from Isaak. Unfortunately, he hadn't even started them.

'I forget your order,' he mumbled sleepily. 'What was it?'

I tried to impress upon him the urgency of the situation, but he remained impassive. 'Do not worry,' he said. 'One man, he is coming.'

Sure enough, one man did come, but he didn't do anything, so I stopped the order. Isaak promptly gave me a new name – Mister Order Cancel Man – and sank into a major sulk.

'Well, that's it.' I told Tim. 'Time to go home. Time to confront Spud with the news that I've cancelled all his orders and won't be letting him go buying again.'

Tim raised an eyebrow. 'Rather you than me,' he replied. 'I'd hold back with that second piece of news if I were you.'

I was defiant. Spud had blown his last chance. Not only had he ruined both our reputations in India, but my new title of 'Mister Order Cancel Man' stuck in my craw. I hadn't deserved it; the name belonged to Spud. And now, after all those cancelled orders and Spud's insane assault on Isaak, no one (bar Satish) would make any more clothing for us.

Back in England, I stormed into Spud's office and found him sitting behind a new director's desk, sniffing trails of coke off its shiny veneer. 'I'm chasing an outline of my van!' he said, giggling insanely. 'I'm down to the last wheel!'

I rattled off my carefully rehearsed speech of complaint, but Spud wasn't listening. He was off in a private world where he was a little Napoleon and everyone else was his lackey troops.

'Who do you think you *are?*' he asked me with a mad cackle. 'Without me, you're *nothing!*'

I eyed him doubtfully and left the room.

The final straw, when it came, was brutal. Shortly after my return, I went out in the van and took a record £12,000 in a single week.

Not to be outdone, Spud went out the following week and also came back with £12,000. It was such a coincidence that I decided to investigate. And what I found out, after much questioning, shocked me to the core. Judging competition to be more important than partnership, Spud had sold the entire contents of his van to another wholesaler – and for a lot less than it had cost to buy them.

'Half that stuff was mine!' I raged. 'And you sold it at a loss?'

'No, I didn't,' Spud replied, smirking. 'You're just being paranoid.'

'Oh yeah? Then why is your van empty?'

'I'm having it cleaned.'

'And the contents?'

'None of your business.' Suddenly he was on the offensive. He narrowed his eyes and leaned towards me. 'I've been asking around, and I've found out you're the one who's been giving people big discounts. I always wondered how you sold more than me. Now I know. You've been undercutting me for years!'

'So this is payback?'

'Call it a lesson,' Spud said stonily. 'Nobody fucks with *me* and gets away with it.'

'Okay,' I said. 'Fine. But you've cut your own throat in the process. That van had over fifty grand of stuff in it.'

He shrugged. 'So what? A lesson is a lesson.'

I went very quiet inside. 'This is the end of the road,' I said. 'You've just lost yourself a partner.'

'Yeah, right,' mocked Spud, completely nonplussed. 'You leave, and you're good as dead.'

'Really? Is that a threat?'

Another shrug. 'Call it what you want. But you're not

going anywhere.'

I turned on my heel and strode out of Spud's house. I would have kept going, marching straight out of Spud's life, too, but I couldn't. The company chequebook was still in Spud's hands. And since all our money was tied up in stock, it would be many months before Spud could afford to buy me out.

So I did the only thing I could do. I went back to work with Spud—for Spud, in effect—until two things forced a final separation.

First, I learnt my mother was sick.

Second, I met Madge.

₹

Chapter 21

Plague? What Plague?

On 1st September 1996, I finally split with Spud. I stuck around long enough, on Spud's insistence, to train up his only long-time 'friend', Fat Pete, so he could take over my job. I then endured a long week of humiliation, during which I phoned Spud every day to ask for my thirty grand 'severance pay.' And every day I was cynically fobbed off. On one occasion I even heard Tim, my one remaining ally, audibly snickering in the background at my pathetic, begging calls. But by the end of the week I had my money at last, and I was free of the whole sorry mess.

I was sad it had come to this, but I hadn't had a choice. My sanity was at stake. During the final six months of our partnership, as I burnt rubber to earn my precious exit cheque, I had slaved twelve hours a day, seven days a week, and was close to a breakdown. And in all that time Spud had been looking over my shoulder, pushing me on, defying me to leave, yet wanting me to stay. He was now playing the jilted lover: harsh, unforgiving, and full of scorn. But at the same time he left the back door open should I ever decide to return.

I could not return. Five long years of non-stop wheeling and dealing had finally caught up with me, and I needed a break. I also gave Spud the one reason for getting out that Spud could understand – my mother had just been diagnosed with cancer, and I wanted to spend more time with her.

But the real reason was the drugs. I could not return to work with a partner who was falling apart before my eyes. Spud was a shadow of his former self, no longer fat and healthy, but pale and gaunt; no longer in charge of his emotions, but wild and irrational, like a simmering volcano. It was almost too painful to watch. I tried—only once—to stop it.

'What's with the coke, the Es, and the endless parties?' I asked. 'I'm doing all the work here, and you're just sitting behind that desk, filling your nose with crap!'

'Mind your own fucking business!' Spud growled. His eyes were rolling like deranged marbles as he said this, and his mouth was ringed with dry spittle. 'Somebody's got to be on the ball here. And with you sabotaging all my plans, cancelling my orders in India, and cutting my prices in the UK, it sure ain't fucking *you!*'

I did not try again.

I had no clear plans for the future other than wanting to take my mother to India while her cancer was in brief remission. I wanted to share the most important place in my life with the most important person, and for the two of us to enjoy one last holiday together.

I also—and this was a very secret agenda—still craved my mother's sanction. I was fed up with being told I could 'do better' for myself. I wanted her to see that though I had never become the doctor or architect she had expected of me, I was no longer a lowly 'barrow boy' on a London market stall. Now I was a man of substance in a foreign land.

The holiday couldn't happen just yet, though. Nasty rumours had started trickling in about India, and I decided to put my mum's ticket on hold. I flew to Delhi alone, and during the flight over I scanned the papers for more news. That's when I realised I really shouldn't have been going there at all.

India had fallen victim to a lot of recent flooding, I learnt, due to an abnormal monsoon. It had been this, more than anything else, which had brought rats and a plague to Gujarat. The plague had spread to the capital, and everybody was wandering around the streets wearing white masks, looking haunted. This explained the mysterious fax Spud had received from Gordhan, saying his consignment had been delayed 'due to action of plague.' For once it wasn't just an excuse, but the truth. Indeed, on the very same day that I booked my flight into India, all flights out of India were indefinitely suspended.

My arrival at the Oberoi in Delhi caused quite a stir. All foreign reservations had been cancelled, I was informed, so I had the whole hotel to myself.

'Big fuss over nothing!' complained Mr Bhatia, the manager. 'Only fifty people die, but everyone want to quit India. They come my hotel, take all my guests, and send them back to their country.'

'Who does?'

'The government. They do not want any dead foreigners on their hands.'

'Isn't the plague serious, then?' I asked.

He rolled his eyes. 'Oh yes, it is "serious", but only because the press make it serious. All media is going crazy, shouting "Plague this!" and "Plague that!" It will kill tourism in this country, you know. It is "storm in a teacup", as you British say, and it will cost us for many years to come!'

To date there had actually only been two deaths in Delhi, but fears of an epidemic were rife. Even now, with the schools and hospitals cautiously reopening, the streets were almost empty. They were also, I noticed as I taxied into town, incredibly clean. In only three weeks the garbage trucks—working flat out for once—had managed to remove fifty years of accumulated rubbish.

There was not even one other foreign buyer in Paharganj. In fact, there were no other foreigners at all. The only activity along Main Bazar was a single huddle of garlic sellers hunched under a large umbrella, hiding from the hot autumn sun. Most shops and eateries were closed until further notice, and all the street-touts had taken to sleeping or playing cards in back alleys. Paharganj, like the rest of Delhi, had become a ghost town. Only the occasional barking dog or tinkling bicycle bell disturbed the eerie feeling of post-nuclear calm.

I couldn't help but think that this situation was a buyer's paradise. I knew I was callous thinking that way, but with no traffic on the roads, no shops clogged with foreigners, and nobody else competing for goods, I had India all to myself. It was a golden opportunity, and I would be a fool to pass it up.

But I was cautious. Before committing myself I decided to check out Jaipur, to see if it was the same story there. After all, I was supposed to be 'retired.' I couldn't afford to take any chances.

I needn't have worried. In Chameliwala market I came upon a very happy Gordhan.

'Flag sell! Flag sell!' he said, hooking a short chubby arm around my neck. 'Hee, hee, hee!'

'Flag sell?' I repeated, puzzled, and then, 'Oh! You mean *plague* sale!'

'Yes, yes!' I let him guide me firmly into his warehouse. 'Flag sell, just for you!'

'But haven't you heard? I'm no longer in business. I'm here on holiday.'

'Yes, yes,' persisted Gordhan. 'First make business, *then* take holiday!'

There was no point arguing with him. In Jaipur, as in Delhi, I was the sole buyer in town, surrounded by masses of shops desperate to sell me stuff at rock bottom prices. I felt like a kid let loose in a candy store. Excited, I wired home for more money, then stopped.

Spud wouldn't like this one bit.

Along with this thought came another: 'Who cares what Spud likes?'

It wasn't as though I owed Spud any loyalty. He had used and abused me for years. Plus Spud had bought me out real cheap: just thirty grand for a company worth millions. I still had a few customers of my own back home, I figured, shops that wouldn't deal with Spud under any circumstances. So why shouldn't I start buying again?

Gordhan was keen for cash. So keen for cash in fact that he let me go through Spud's entire shipment, a shipment for which Spud hadn't yet paid. With a wide grin and open arms, he invited me to pick out all the best pieces. Girish did the same with Spud's jewellery, also not yet paid for. They stopped short of selling me all Spud's goods when I casually remarked that my mother was coming to visit in a few days. This piece of news had both men inexplicably jumping for joy.

Prompted by their reaction, I picked up the phone and rang back home. It was my mother's birthday, 20th October, and to commemorate it I told her she was coming to India after all. I did not mention the word plague. My stepfather would never have let her on the plane.

While awaiting her arrival, I briefly visited Ram in Pushkar to arrange a camel trek for her. 'This is not a problem,' he solemnly assured me. 'I will make one special safari for

Mama! One special camel also!'

He then guided me out of his shop to show me his new sign. It read:

Ram's Camel Adventures!
We enjoy people!
We presents the Thar Desert!
The Thar Desert is a world of its own
— an unrelived ocean of sand dotted with
beautiful dune and spotted with xeropaytic shrubbery!

Amused, I asked Ram what "xeropaytic shrubbery" was and he said it was shrubs that mostly lived on a dry diet. He had got this phrase out of an ancient English dictionary, and no amount of persuasion could get him to change it.

I strolled through Pushkar market, once again struck by the absence of white faces. Even the Israelis were gone, packed off to Delhi the previous week by the tourist police. All the shopkeepers were crying.

'No business, no profit, no life!' complained Satish, and he reflected the sentiments of everyone in town.

The last time I had seen Pushkar this quiet, I reflected, was when Rajiv Gandhi had been assassinated in 1991. Flanked by two neat rows of turbaned soldiers, some of the great man's ashes had been brought up the long market street to be deposited in the holy lake. Only George and I, emerging from Mendu's shop after hours of checking silk, had witnessed the event. Every other tourist had been chucked onto a bus and sent out of the country.

Rajiv was the best Prime Minister India ever had, but he was never long for this world. Like his namesake, the Mahatma, he tried to change millennia of class prejudice within the space of a few years. After defying the caste system and trying to give land and votes to both villagers and untouchables, his assassination had been a sad inevitability.

I did not enjoy the quiet of the street for long. The news that I had gone out of business spread like wildfire, but none of the Pushkar shops could believe it. The only reason anyone went out of business, in their opinion, was that one had too much money to know what to do with it.

I found this out when Satish drove me out to an empty wasteland on the outskirts of town and proposed that he and I build a hotel there. He was closely followed by Ram, who suggested opening a chain of joint handicrafts shops. Finally there was Girish, who dragged me to one side as soon as I arrived back in Jaipur and tried to interest me in co-owning Jaipur's first ever 'disco bar.' Each of these strange projects would have required an initial investment from me of at least £20,000, which, unknown to anyone, was about all I had left in the world.

It was now time to meet my mother, and I went to see travel desk Deepak, to prepare for the nine hour drive from Pushkar to the Delhi airport.

'I want a good car this time,' I told him. 'I do not want my mother going to Gujarat!'

Deepak laughed, a deep baritone sound, and gave me an Ambassador taxi which was quite literally tyred-out. The front nearside tyre was more bald than Spud's head. 'Why don't you change that tyre for this one?' I suggested, pointing at the brand new tyre lying in the boot, but Deepak just giggled. 'After,' he said.

'After what?' I barked. 'After we've crashed and died?'

'This is not a problem you need to concern yourself,' Deepak said confidently. 'You have number one car!'

Two hours out of Jaipur I became very concerned. The bald tyre expired with a loud pop, and we skidded over to the hard shoulder. The driver laughed merrily to himself and exchanged the dead tyre for an even balder one which had been cleverly secured beneath the undercarriage by a piece of string. The new tyre—the one still lying in the boot—was obviously only there for show.

Thirty-two minutes later, the replacement tyre exploded, instantly wiping the grin off the driver's face. He was now forced to use the good tyre, a necessity which plunged him into a deep gloom. Then he started wrestling with the gearstick, and I suspected a new problem. Despite wiggling with and shoving at the gear shift, he could not locate any other gear but first. The car crawled along at a funereal pace for ten minutes until he finally juggled the stick up to third. At this point, just as we'd managed to establish a sensible speed, we ran over a pig. Rather, the pig ran under us—then it scurried out the other side, miraculously having escaped injury.

We rolled into Delhi around dusk, still cruising in third gear. The first thing the driver did on arrival was to buy two more bald tyres. The first thing I did was ring the Oberoi and book a different car. I had just spotted my driver putting the 'show' tyre back in the boot...and fixing another suicide one in its place.

₹

Chapter 22

Mother India

A small, familiar figure emerged from the throng of new arrivals at Delhi airport, waving an unnecessary umbrella.

It was my mother, and she was on a roll.

She excitedly introduced me to three total strangers she had met on the plane, and then she found a hole in my jumper and lunged into her bag for a sewing kit to fix it on the spot.

I guided her gently but firmly into the waiting taxi – her chattering all the while – and took her straight off to Jaipur. I couldn't *wait* to introduce her to Gordhan.

If she was tired from the flight, she certainly didn't show it. By the time we reached Dudu, the midway food-stop, she had fired off so many questions to the driver – about his life, his hopes, and his dreams – that he had become positively entranced by her. As we ground to a halt, he turned to me and said, 'I like your *mummy!*' Then he pointed at her, still beaming away in the back seat, and said, 'You take *my* mummy, I take *your* mummy!'

Well, that shut her up. The prospect of living the rest of her days in some hot and dusty Rajasthani village was so scary that she immediately lay down in the back seat and pretended to sleep.

Six hours down the line in Jaipur, Gordhan stuck his hand out to my mother…and became the surprised recipient of her useless umbrella. She then proceeded to make such a fuss of him, his workers, and his family that they all wanted to be Hungarian. Hungarians, if she was anything to go by, were obviously a lot more fun and well-mannered than any other foreigners they'd come across. They heard her rattle on about exotic places like Budapest and Lake Sopron (where her father had once owned vast lands) and they wanted to relocate there immediately and meet lots of other Hungarians just like her.

'She is honoured *guest!*' protested Gordhan as we made to leave. 'Your family is *my* family, and family guest *not* leave! She stay *my* house! Son Girish move *downstairs*!'

Once again, I had to remind my mother not to be too friendly with the locals. They would only keep wanting to adopt her.

'Why you not bring mummy *before*?' said Gordhan, his triple fat chins wobbling with irritation. 'She is *too* much nice, Frankie, and she is liking India much more than in UK!'

It was a good question, but difficult to explain. The short answer was that my step-father, who was terminally infantilised and couldn't even boil an egg, didn't want her going anywhere. It was only her imminent demise that had finally persuaded him, after years of fruitless requests, to let her go for a couple of weeks and fly to India.

The long answer was that my mother had too much invested in England to ever want to leave it. She had fled over the mountains with her father in 1945, carrying the family rugs and silver, to escape an advancing Russian army. The Russians had already seized the ancestral estates – worth millions – and were on the hunt for anyone who'd held political office in wartime Hungary. My grandfather, who had been a key part of the cabinet, had been a prime target. Later on, when things quietened down, he'd cautiously returned to Budapest as an architect, to help rebuild the city's bombed-out factories along modern (German) lines.

My mother, on the other hand, settled down in London. She liked it there, especially its 'interesting weather', and began attending English evening classes. It was here that she met my real father, a Polish lawyer who had never got to practice law because the Russians had stuck him in an icy gulag for four long years. By 1947, when he was liberated by the British and came to England, he had lost all of his hair – most of his health too – and was a nervous wreck. All the more surprising, then, that this small anxious man who liked to dress up like Humphrey Bogart – complete with a low trilby hat and a long trench-coat – managed to charm my mother, who could have been a model. Whenever I saw pictures of her in her youth, I was struck by her perfect smile, her perfect figure, and her perfect pile of jet-black hair. 'Just like Jackie Onassis!' I would marvel. 'What on earth made her marry that bald little Pole?'

But marry him she had. The frail, failed lawyer made her laugh, she said. He had a dry sardonic wit and a lively imagination, and he could mimic all the great screen comics, from Chaplin to Hancock to Sellers, to perfection. 'Hardly a day went past,' she once told me, 'without me in stitches!'

The first two heart attacks didn't kill him, but the third one did. I was just two at the time, and my mother not yet thirty. We had grieved together in a small one-bed flat in Balham and then, when I was old enough, we started travelling.

I directly inherited the travel bug from my mother. She took me on a long series of holidays all around Europe – a different country every summer – until, quite suddenly, she re-married a totally unadventurous man and had her wings clipped for the next 25 years. I hadn't been expecting this. I'd expected her to marry John, a handsome civil engineer who wanted to take us both to India. I was enthralled by this idea – I liked John, and it would have got me to India 20 years earlier – but my mother thought otherwise. 'You're going to have a *proper* education in England,' she told me, 'and I'm going to make sure of it!'

And that's what she did. With John out of the picture (gone to India), I got Bert, the ultimate English patriarch. Bert liked staying at home, watching sports on TV, and being served his meals on time. Bert did *not* like holidays, going outdoors, or being contradicted. His house was his castle and his word was law. Bert may have loved my mother, but he disliked me on sight. I hated watching sports, ate when I felt like it, and talked back all the time. More to the point, Bert sensed that he could never supplant me in my mother's affections. He would only ever be second best.

Bert started out nice and friendly, but then got progressively more unhinged. He didn't like it when he realised his new wife loved me more than him. His verbal abuse of me started early, and became more and more hysterical. And as it did so, as his childish jealousy overcame him, Bert unwittingly isolated himself. My mum and I began staying up all night – her sipping martinis, me listening to endless stories of forgotten Hungarian relatives. Our nocturnal mutterings and hysterical laughter drove poor Bert crazy. Every night, he would charge down the stairs shouting, 'What time do you call *this,* woman? Come to *bed*!' – only to be fobbed off with her sweet smile and soft reply, 'I won't be a minute, darling!'

She never went, of course. Night time was our time, her time and mine, when we could travel wherever we wanted, in our minds and imaginations.

In India, free of Bert and all restrictions, I'd seen my mother as she used to be – gay, flirtatious, full of fun and frivolity. I'd known that she would love India: it had the same charm, curiosity and innocence that she herself possessed. She was no beauty any more, the cancer had seen to that, but the light within her was undimmed. If anything, with her arrival in India, it glowed brighter than ever. It was as though, sensing her time running out, she was determined to make the most of every remaining moment.

*

Our arrival in Pushkar the next day was the big event of the year. Everyone knew we were coming, and no sooner had my mother got out of the taxi than Jagat Singh, the most influential man in town, appeared and festooned her head with sweet-smelling garlands of jasmine and frangipani. He welcomed her into his 'humble' 4-star hotel and introduced her, in turn, to every member of the local royal family. He then ushered her, through a swaying crowd, into the glitzily decorated restaurant and plied her with a huge banquet of local delicacies. He had heard, through me, that my mother knew her way around a kitchen – that she had once cooked for the likes of Churchill and Mountbatten – and he was desperate to impress her. During a brief interlude, Manish, the kitchen manager, sang her a plaintive tune of his own composition – very sweet – while Norath, the reception guy, danced up and down in the foreground, clapping his hands together in glee. Everyone but *everyone* wanted to have their photograph taken with her, and it was only when my old friend Ram, the designated master of ceremonies, appeared with a camel that she was finally whisked away into the desert for a bit of peace and quiet.

Nick and Anna joined us on the trek, and it was a good thing too. My poor mum had been so overwhelmed by her reception that she was crying uncontrollably and needed calming down. Gently swaying on top of a camel helped steady her nerves, but it was Nick who put things into perspective for her. 'Indians have a thing about mothers anyway,' he quietly informed her, 'but your son has been writing about Pushkar and doing business here for ten years, so of course the whole town wants to see you. You're an *extra special* mother!'

To drive the point home, Ram then kicked off about me buying him three camels, and giving half the town's tailors work and money, so that 'the name of Kusy will never be forgotten in this world.'

I'm not good at this kind of thing. In fact, I found the whole business just plain embarrassing. I tried to hide, but my mother followed me onto one of the dunes, where I was doing my evening prayers. She sat beside me, waited for me to finish, then—for the first time in my life—said she was proud of me. Somehow, after decades of disapproval, I had finally won her respect.

We held hands a while, and then, in the silence that followed the sun slowly disappearing over the horizon, she said, 'I'm going to miss you.' I held her tight and whispered, 'I'm going to miss *you* too.' Then we cried for a bit, and it was as if a large load had been lifted from our hearts. We had spoken the unspoken and had come to terms with it. All that was important now, we both agreed, was that we treasure the time still left to us and simply enjoy the present.

I can't remember much of what came after. I knew that my mother was mobbed in Pushkar – treated like a visiting queen

– and that she spent most of her time there either laughing with joy or weeping with emotion. But apart from a few seconds of video from Nick, when she first mounted her camel, and one faded photograph of her on an elephant, ascending the high Amber Fort in Jaipur, I had no memories at all. Maybe they were too painful, maybe I just blocked them out, but my mind was a complete blank.

The one thing I *do* clearly recall is that when she died, a few short months later, she was still clutching the album of photographs we'd made together in India. I don't know what happened to that album – maybe she took it to the grave with her – but she never let it out of her sight. It had been the twilight highlight of her life, this last holiday together, and it had given her the peace to let go.

₹

Chapter 23

Margreet

Margreet came into my life just as my mother was about to leave it. Tall, blonde and beautiful, she actually reminded me a lot *of* my mother. She had the same perfect teeth, the same vivacity and humour, even the same chattiness and love of travel. She was also a Continental, having been born and brought up in Holland. My mum couldn't believe her luck when Margreet came round to the family house. 'What have we got *here*?' I could hear her thinking. 'Not just smart and good-looking, but *so* well-presented and a university lecturer to boot! Thank *you*, Jesus!'

When we told my mum, a short month later, that we were getting married, she fell quiet for only the second time in her life – the first having been the taxi incident at Dudu. Then she dipped into her handbag, took out a hankie, and wept into it from sheer happiness. Madge and I had sped up the wedding plans, to make sure that she would be able to attend, and she was, for that day at least, all smiles and anticipation.

But then the cancer had returned, and this time it had attacked her spine. She wasn't sure she was going to make the wedding, she said, and she certainly didn't want to be photographed in a wheelchair. Instead, whether by accident or design, she slipped away in her sleep, just nine hours before the nuptials. Did she take too many pills that night? Did she think her work done and her son safely off to the registry office? I would never know.

It was the 31st August 1997 – the day I lost the most important person in my life and gained the next. The only Indian I informed of the event, Gordhan, thought it a highly inauspicious sign and advised that I cancel the wedding forthwith. But it was too late for that. Over a hundred guests were already on their way and the honeymoon – in India, of course – was only two days off.

My mother had timed things to perfection. She knew exactly how long to boil an egg, and she knew exactly when to leave this world – so that I would *have* to get married and be forever looked after by someone else.

*

Suddenly, with my mum's death, I had no family home and no family. While I was away, my step-brother John had sold up and moved his dad to Enfield. All I had left were Anita's cats and a house in Peckham that was in peril. It was in peril because Spud had just discovered that his precious shipment, the one he had ordered from Gordhan, had been sold to me instead.

'You bastard!' he shouted down the phone. 'You said you weren't going back into business. I needed that stuff for a big London show!'

'Well, you should have paid for it then!' I shouted back. 'And I only said I wasn't going back into business with you!'

'Nobody fucks with me and gets away with it!' Spud said again. 'You've just moved up to number one on my death list!'

I recalled a similar warning, issued to the head buyer at Liberty's a few years before, and promptly moved house. Which was just as well, since a week later the new tenant found Spud tinkering with the gas mains, intent on blowing the place up.

Now this *was* serious, and I rang up two of my oldest Buddhist friends – Anna and Brenda – to ask their advice. They both told me the same thing. If I was so worried about Spud, they said, I should chant for Spud's happiness.

'Chant for Spud's happiness?' I scoffed. 'I don't think so. Spud's only going to be happy when I'm dead!'

Then I thought better of it and took their advice on board. I chanted long and hard for Spud's happiness and came up with the perfect solution. If I couldn't make Spud happy by being dead, I would make Spud happy by being as good as dead. I left no trace of my new whereabouts. I changed my bank, my van, my mobile phone, even my appearance.

'If Spud wants to be Mister Incognito,' I decided, 'I can go one better. I can be Mister Invisible!'

With my new contact lenses, my perky Castro hat, and my clean-shaven face, not even my new best friend Justin recognised me.

'Before,' marvelled Justin, 'you looked like a head posing as a journalist. Now, you look like a journalist posing as a head!'

'I can't walk down the road with you anymore!' complained Margreet. 'You look about twelve years old with no beard. I feel like a paedophile!'

Margreet – or Madge, as I came to call her – had a habit of not mincing her words. She also had a fiery temper, like Anita, and a mind of her own. Fortunately, unlike Anita, she was very level-headed, so I felt safe in moving in with her on the other side of London. This temporarily took me off Spud's radar. It also marked a whole new phase in my life. I set up a new company and began taking entire days off. As these days off became entire weekends off, my life slowly fell into a more even rhythm. I was coming to embrace the Buddhist principle of the Middle Way, and with only sixty solid customers to deal with, instead of the numerous time-wasters I'd had with Spud, I could finally strike a balance between work and play.

Only one mystery remained. I needed to know how Spud had managed to run the old company, a huge wholesale empire with an annual turnover of two million pounds, into the ground in only eight short months.

Through hearsay and gossip, I gleaned that my old partner had spent far more time partying than attending to business. He had even brought Ram over from India and introduced him to London's burgeoning rave scene. Nothing apparently gave Spud more pleasure than walking into a strobe-lit nightclub accompanied by a turbaned Rajasthani on crutches. He had somehow persuaded Ram that I was a false friend, that I would abandon him in the same way I had 'abandoned' Spud. When Ram flipped out on some bad pills and got arrested, Spud had apparently taken the same pleasure in putting his disabled pet monkey on a plane back to India. Spud, it seemed, had no truck with losers.

I also learnt that Spud had stopped going to India himself. Instead, he sent out pairs of grungy hippy chicks to check out his clothing. The idea was nothing short of a disaster, since the girls spent all their time getting stoned and doing no work at all. The stuff they did send back had been so rotten that anyone fool enough to buy it never dealt with Spud again.

At last—this was the final irony—all of Spud's staff deserted and came back to me, cap in hand, asking for work.

On Madge's advice, I turned them all away.

₹

Chapter 24

Second Honeymoon

The 24th of January 1998 found me at Delhi airport, anxiously waiting for Madge to fly in from England. We had had a horrid first honeymoon – all tears and misery following on from my mum's death – and this time I was determined to get it right. To make sure, I had completed all my business before she turned up, making a frantic £6000 buy in two days so I could give her my full attention.

After a short wait she turned up, flustered and excited, and introduced me to a couple of Belgians she had met on the plane. It was just like my mother again—but without the umbrella.

'This is what I remember!' exclaimed Madge as we screamed into Delhi in a convoy of buzzing auto-rickshaws. 'It's all coming back to me now!'

'What do you mean?' I said.

'Well, I grew up in North India,' she explained. 'I was here in Delhi, then up in Kashmir as a child. I never thought I'd be coming back thirty years later to find it all so familiar!'

The Oberoi Maidens, the hotel I'd chosen, blew Madge away. She had a thing about art-deco architecture, and she was transported with delight by this imposing, Raj-style structure, with its magnificent pre-war façade and eight acres of emerald green lawns.

'Did you know,' she read excitedly, running her finger down the hotel brochure, 'that the Duke of Windsor stayed here in 1927? And that Edward Lutyens, the architect of New Delhi, lived here while the new city was being built in the '30s?'

I didn't know. I had never bothered to find out. What I did know was that this was the flagship of the Oberoi hotel chain, and that Mr Oberoi himself favoured it over all the others. I also knew that it was the quietest, most hospitable luxury hotel in India.

'It's the staff that does it,' I told Madge. 'They treat you just like family. They're not stuffy or stuck-up at all.'

Anil, my old friend at reception, had put us in the honeymoon suite. The room was so spot-on, so full of colonial charm and splendour, that Madge was in raptures.

'Look at this!' she exclaimed, awestruck. 'Half this stuff belongs in a museum!'

She was so enamoured of the high ballroom ceilings, the regal furnishings, and the luxurious marble bathroom that I hesitated to drag her away. But then I remembered that Satish Agarwal was coming soon to drive us to Pushkar. And I wanted to show Madge all the famous sights of Old Delhi: the majestic Red Fort of Shah Jahan, the teeming markets of Chandni Chowk, and the largest mosque in the country, the Jame Masjid. For just this day, we forgot we had seen it all before—in my case many times. We took each other's hands, stepped into the crowded street and became normal tourists doing the standard whirlwind tour of the capital.

*

It was gone noon the next day when Satish arrived. He shifted from one foot to the other in the hallway outside our room, apologizing, saying he would have been earlier but he had had a slight 'accident' on the road and had just finished scraping a dead goat off his windshield. He was about to say something else when I opened the door and ushered him inside the vast suite. Eyes wide with wonder, Satish gave a long, low whistle.

'All this for you?' he asked reverentially. 'Are you now UK ambassador?'

I chuckled. 'Not yet,' I said. 'This is special for honeymoon people!'

'Congratulations!' said Satish, seizing and pumping Madge's hand. 'I hope you have a very *vigorous* night!'

Sanjay, Satish's younger brother, was right behind him. He didn't say a word but watched in silence as Satish sank contentedly into a plush leather sofa. Then—after a quick nod from me—he dived into the opulent bathroom for an hour long shower. After he was done, the brothers went off shopping like two excited schoolboys, then returned a while later carrying presents for their mother and wives. Delhi was like the Big Apple to them. They couldn't get enough of it. By the time they had all clambered into the van and headed back to Pushkar, the brothers were in a transport of ecstasy. Sanjay was in the back, caressing his new electric mixer, while Satish sat up front, happily humming Hindi tunes and drumming his fingers on the dashboard. From time to time, barely able to contain his excitement, he turned around and beamed back at us with his fat Omar Sharif face.

'*HAPPY?*' he roared. 'You *HAPPY? NICE* here! Yes, *BEAUTIFUL.* Oh *YES!* Good, *GOOD!*'

I couldn't help nodding. Satish's enthusiasm was genuinely contagious. Five years before, however, it had been a very different story. Back then, I told Madge, Satish had been like a man possessed – so urgent, so driven, so desperate to get my business that I'd had to grab him by the shoulders to shut him up.

'Look here, Satish,' I'd told him, 'how can you take orders when you don't listen long enough to write them down?'

Now, five years later, Satish whipped out a new ballpoint as if on cue, and started putting pen to paper.

'Oh good!' praised Madge. 'Writing everything down now!'

'Yes,' said Satish, looking pleased. 'Writing is better than *thinking!*'

Satish was at a complete loss as to where to fit Madge into the Indian caste system – until, that is, he learnt that she was a teacher. Not just any teacher, mind you, but a university lecturer. After that, he treated her like a princess. This was because teachers (like priests) belonged to the top caste of Indian society, way above businessmen like Satish, and were accorded the highest respect.

'In England is opposite!' Madge shouted over the engine noise. 'Teachers there are very low profession. Too much work, too little money, and thought to be teachers because they can do nothing else.'

'Really?' Satish was incredulous. 'England sound crazy! I no go there!'

After this last burst of conversation, he fell silent. I had given him a Hindi music tape to play on the van's stereo, and all we could see from the back seat was his silhouette clapping in time to the music and wobbling his head. The only moments of quiet happened when he stopped the cassette, then rewound or forwarded it for no obvious reason. So we enjoyed three hours of disjointed, blaring music, with loud clacks in between which ensured we never dropped off.

The driver, meanwhile, was so distracted by the whole experience he was in constant danger of hitting things. It was even worse when it got dark. He was so blinded by the headlights of oncoming trucks that he couldn't see and began aiming the van at roadside trees. The final leg to Pushkar was a nightmare, with the driver hunched over his wheel, peering myopically down the highway, and Satish bobbing and weaving in the front seat, happily gurgling to Hindi tunes, completely oblivious to the danger.

'This driver I have for eight years,' he said at one point. 'I like him because he is not dead.'

*

So at last I managed to get Madge to Pushkar – to where I should have taken her, if I'd had any sense, on our first honeymoon. Here I had friends, practically family, and she would have been guaranteed a good time.

Madge loved Pushkar, and Pushkar loved Madge. From the moment she arrived, she was treated like royalty, just like my mother. Jagat Singh rolled out the red carpet again, and crowds of adoring locals crammed into the Palace Hotel to pelt her with flowers and greetings. Faced by such unexpected attention, it took her half an hour to reach our room.

'What was that all about?' she asked, mystified.

'You'll see,' I said, grinning. 'That was just the start!'

And so it was, for as we proceeded into town all the traders sussed who Madge was and began giving her presents in the hope of getting my future business. Inside an hour she was so loaded down with scarves, shawls, blankets, and wooden puppets that she could barely see past her nose.

'What's going on?' she demanded, her eyes somewhat glazed over. 'They're greeting you like some visiting Viceroy and me as your queen! You're strolling ahead as though nothing is happening, and I'm trailing behind like a Muslim wife!'

I laughed. 'Are you really complaining? You've got more stuff in your arms than I have in my warehouse!'

In the centre of the market, just as we were unloading Madge's loot onto a roadside trolley, we were accosted by Mister Bullshit.

'Thank you very much, sir!' crooned Lalit Jain, vigorously shaking my hand. 'You are very kind, sir! I have got only one heart, but if I had two hearts I would thank you even more—double, double!'

Lalit was now the top moneychanger in town. He was eager for me to see his new shop sign, which read: 'Easy Cash – By Authority of Government.'

'It's about time you got authorised,' I teased. 'You've been unauthorised for ten years!'

'India is great, man!' said Lalit, nodding sagely. 'Better than anything! Now I give official Encashment Certificate, so more customer, more business!'

We were rescued by Satish, who gave Madge a beautiful Kashmiri shawl and brought her home to meet his family. The house was a simple affair, rather ramshackle, with gay garlanded shrines to various gods parked in every corner. Inside, Sanjay's wife (yes, he had finally been allowed to marry) prepared us a pure vegetarian meal. Satish's two young sons took an instant shine to Madge and kept her occupied by asking excited questions.

'It was nice,' she commented later, 'to get away from all the western tourists and sample a piece of real Indian life!'

The one disappointment of the day was Ram. I had been looking forward to introducing him to Madge and to treating her to one of his famous camel treks. But he was nowhere to be found. According to Himmat, the manager of the Venus, Ram had returned from England 'a little crazy.' Spud had apparently laid a lot of drugs on him and filled his head with delusions of grandeur. Thus it was that Ram had been jailed recently for scamming $10,000 off Eri, his loyal Japanese girlfriend, after promising to marry her. When he married a local Indian girl instead and the liaison with Eri had broken down, he refused to give her money back, and the whole of Pushkar had rejoiced in the scandal.

'Hello, Mister Japanese!' they'd shouted at him for weeks afterwards, and though he'd quickly bribed his way out of jail, he had been forced to leave town until all the gossip died down.

He was back in town now, but all attempts to set up a rendezvous—with his younger brother R.J. acting as go-between—met with failure. Ram stood us up twice that evening, leaving me both confused and angry. I could only presume that he had been too ashamed to face me, or that Spud had screwed up his mind so much that he had forgot his loyalties. Whatever it was, I had to apologise to Madge, saying that my 'best friend in Pushkar' was now a thief and a coward.

₹

Chapter 25

Mister Magic Trouser Man

The next day Nick and Anna blew into town, and the four of us went on a camel trek into the desert. In the absence of Ram, his brother R.J. did the honours.

'Today is special day!' R.J. declared with a twinkle in his eyes.

'How's that, then?' I asked.

'Today is 26th January. Day of our Independence!'

'Is that good?'

'It is better than good! It is *fan*tastic! No bloody British for fifty years!'

'But *I'm* British!'

'No matter,' R.J. added conspiratorially. 'You are always welcome to come *back*. Especially to my silver shop!'

Madge liked Nick, saying, 'Under that quiet exterior, there's a wicked sense of humour,' but at first she wasn't sure what to make of Anna.

'She's the bright bubbly one,' she concluded at last. 'She tried to take me under her wing, but had no idea of how to talk to Europeans. As soon as she learnt I was Dutch, and thus foreign, she started speaking to me in the same pigeon-English she reserves for Indians, saying stuff like 'Where you coming from? Oh, much much far!' She obviously thinks 'foreign' equals Indian!'

The camel safari was a great success. Madge didn't know how to get onto a camel, so she stood awhile, stroking it cautiously. Nick strode over and took the reins in one hand.

'You can't move a camel by being nice to it,' he told her. 'You have to do like the Indians do, and bark *"Jttt! Jttt!"* at it with attitude!'

This was Madge's first time on a camel, and she had a wonderful time. She particularly enjoyed the peacefulness of the desert, a stark contrast to the hullabaloo of the market town. While Nick galloped on ahead, doing his Lawrence of Arabia bit, a small child held the lead of Madge's camel and guided it slowly forward until she fell into a peaceful, quite uncharacteristic, trance. Then came a sudden thunderstorm, a stunning firework show of flashing lightning and dark rumbling clouds. We holed up in a low concrete shelter in the middle of the desert to watch the display. Nick wanted to play charades, but since Madge didn't know what charades was, we entertained her with stories of Pushkar people instead.

'Have you met Mister Magic Trouser Man yet?' asked Nick. 'His real name's Pawan, and he has this little clothing shop close to the Brahma temple. I bought some trousers off him one day but had to go back because they were too long. "No problem," he said, and whipped out a pair of scissors. He sheared about six inches off the bottom and handed them back to me, saying, "Look, magic!"'

'Did they fit?' Madge asked, laughing.

'Oh yes, he'd magicked them perfectly. But the very next day when I went back, he had no trousers at all. He wasn't even wearing any. Instead, anticipating my needs, he wore only a long woollen jacket over bare legs. He had his scissors ready handy, ready to 'magic' the jacket, but his wife dragged him off the street for public indecency.'

'Pushkar is full of strange stuff,' agreed Anna with a giggle. 'We were woken up this morning by a loud banging outside our room. Nick thought it was another beggar asking for money, so he flung open the door and laid into this guy, shouting, "We've had enough of you people hassling us for rupees! Why don't you beg somewhere else?" Imagine his embarrassment when he recognised our landlord, who had only called to collect the rent!'

'Then there's our old pal, Mendu,' continued Nick. 'I saw George in the market earlier, and he was hassling Mendu over his escalating silk prices. This went on for quite some time before Mendu completely lost it. He jumped up, waved a silk dress in George's face, and said in that high, whiny voice of his: "Nick pay … Spud pay … now *you* pay!"'

'My personal favourite,' I added, 'is Sunny, Mr Bullshit's brother, who's gone into the cloth business. Not altogether a wise decision this, since he's colour blind. One of the main reasons Spud went bust apparently was that he sent two hippy chicks to buy tie-dye clothing for him, and the two of them sent Sunny off to Delhi to buy a load of blue and purple fabric for it. But Sunny returned with a truck full of brilliant pinks, oranges and yellows instead. When Spud rang from the UK to berate him for his stupidity, he said simply, "I am black and white only, like TV!"'

A day or so later, I took Madge to the top of the high Savitri temple then down again by way of the famous Brahma temple.

'It's not much to look at,' I apologised. 'But it *is* the only one in India!'

'No, it's not!' she argued. 'What about the one in

178

Mahabilapuram? The hotel manager told us about it while we were on honeymoon, but you were so depressed we walked straight past it!'

That stopped me. 'Really? How embarrassing! All these years I've been telling people that Brahma has only one home in India, and now he has two? What on earth was he doing down in Mahabilapuram?'

'I don't know,' Madge said with a shrug. 'Sunbathing?'

If Madge was unimpressed by the Brahma temple, she was more than impressed by the Pushkar Posse. In one short year, since my last visit, it had expanded exponentially. So many buyers were now in town, as well as friends of buyers, that the Venus restaurant simply couldn't keep up with all of them. Himmat, the new manager, dashed back and forth, trying to seat them all, and eventually came up with a massive fold-out table usually reserved for marriage parties.

'Wow!' declared Madge. 'Twenty-seven hippies sitting at a round table. It's like a scene out of Camelot!"

'Wow!' echoed the Venus's crazy new waiter. 'Too many people! *Wow!'*

'Have you met Mister Wow?' Nick asked. 'His real name is Vinod, but he starts or ends every sentence with the word "Wow"!'

'Wow! Coffee?' asked Vinod. 'Full wow coffee! Take no milk and wow is free!'

Nick gave him his order, but Wow didn't go away. He just stood at the vast table, staring transfixed at the pips rising and falling in my lemon soda.

'Wow!' he declared reverentially. 'Many times up down! Inside magic! Double wow lemon drink!'

'What did you do, Frank?' called over Nick. 'Put too much sugar in again?'

'Yeah man, it nearly—wow—exploded!'

On the way home, Madge gave me a big hug.

'What's that for?' I said.

'That's for making the effort. This honeymoon has been a lot more fun than the first one. When are we coming back?'

On our last day in Pushkar we bade our farewells. Nick and Anna said they would visit in London, and Susie turned up to apologise for her earlier absence. She had been busy with baby number three, she said, but would give us a proper welcome whenever we returned. That was, she added, unless Raju's UK visa finally came through and she made it back to Dagenham.

George we found in a sorry state, though still performing. He was recovering from a severe bout of dysentery, brought on by eating food from dishes washed in polluted lake water. We left him strumming on his ukelele and crooning 'My Sweet Lord' with two freaks in the Sunset Cafe. Apart from the tightly-crossed legs, we wouldn't have guessed he was sick at all.

Our final call was Satish, who was in his shop with his new line of blankets which he called 'Lover Mattresses'. He was selling them hand-over-fist to young Indian honeymooners. Satish was sad to see Madge go. When asked why, he replied that since she had spent three years in India as a child, she had a 'calm and serene mind.'

Little did he know.

₹

Chapter 26

Madge's 64-Million-Dollar Question

Back home again, I was forced to take stock. Not just of my business, but of life in general.

I had been so busy to-ing and fro-ing between India and England that I had somehow lost sight of my goals.

'What *are* your goals?' Madge now asked me. 'You say you're a Buddhist, but you can't sleep, you can't relax, and when you're not busy working you're on the phone to India ordering more stuff to make you even more busy. What's it all *for?*'

It was a good question, and one for which I had no answer. I suspected it might have had something to do with death, for there had been so many losses in my life lately: first my mother, then my stepfather, finally my Buddhist mentor, Dick Causton. In reaction, I had thrown myself into work and was now killing myself simply for work's sake.

Ironically, I hadn't had this problem when I'd been with Spud. Spud had enough vision, enough goals, for the both of us. He had also had a way of putting things that switched on a five-letter word in my head, one that totally fitted in with Thatcher's New Britain – Greed. If big bankers were paying themselves huge bonuses every year, Spud had lectured me, what was wrong with greed? Evidently, greed was good. After all, the whole country was succumbing to it. As revenues from newly found North Sea oil rolled in, as the huge war debt owed to America was finally paid off, England was back in the black. The buzzword was *spend, spend, spend,* and the age of the credit card was born. Ushered in on this new wave of consumerist optimism was a new wave of shops offering unlimited credit, and Spud had been right there waiting for them.

'It's like a giant playground full of cash!' Spud had pronounced. 'All we have to do is reach down and pick it up!'

But then Spud had made his million rupees, and several more million rupees on top of those, and only one thing had made him happy: dropping a wad of cash on the floor of pubs, then—just as someone was about to pick it up—snatching it back again on the end of a piece of string. He had only ever permitted himself one luxury: a brand new Mercedes Benz which was purposefully scratched—the day after he bought it—by some hoodie he had upset at a gas station.

Never once had Spud considered Madge's 64-million dollar question: What was it all *for?*

In the Buddhist scheme of things, I decided, nothing was worth doing unless one enjoyed it and created value from it. If there was a profit to be made, well, that was a bonus.

I returned to my wholesale business with a new determination: I would stop treating customers as customers; I would create value by making friends with them.

When I'd been with Spud, I had worked with over a hundred customers, from the grungy, tattooed owner of a shady head shop, to the pristine, perm-haired manageress of a high-street boutique. Befriending them had been more difficult than I had expected. For one thing, despite my best efforts, they kept on calling me a 'rep.'

'I can't deal with these people,' I had complained to Spud. 'I walk in the door and they say, "Oh, another rep." Who am I representing? Myself? I'm not a lowly fifteen per cent agent. I'm a director of my own company!'

Spud sneered. 'Oh, get over it! They're wankers. Just follow the money!'

That had been easy for Spud. No shopkeeper had ever called him a 'rep.' They were just grateful when he left.

My solution had been more subtle. If anyone called me a rep or ignored me, I went out into the street, hung cheap clothing on the side of my van, and started selling it in full view of the enraged shopkeeper. This tactic didn't make me any friends, but it weeded out a lot of people who didn't want my friendship.

I started weeding out customers as soon as I'd got shot of Spud. The first to go were the cheats and non-payers, starting with the girl from Durham who never paid for the box of clothing I'd sent her the day before my wedding, and the couple from King's Lynn who took advantage of my good nature and ripped me off for five grand worth of jewellery.

Next to go were the time wasters. These consisted of anyone who forgot I was coming, phoned to cancel me at the last minute, or spent hours choosing a single dress or pair of earrings. A typical such time waster was Sarah from Twickenham, who kept me hanging for a year to prevent me from selling to anyone else in her area, then bought off someone else who was more expensive.

'You've got too much stock,' had been her lame excuse. 'I haven't got time to look through it all anymore.'

Finally, there were the rude bastards. Not just 'rep' callers, but people who enjoyed insulting me and watching me suffer.

People like Doug in Cheltenham, who 'helped' me reverse my van into a brand new Jag, then jumped up and down in the back of the van until the Jag's front bumper fell off.

'You really shouldn't have done that!' Doug cried gleefully as police and traffic wardens swarmed around me.

That left about 40 customers with whom I *could* deal with and keep my self-respect. I gave respect to all my suppliers in India, no matter how often they let me down. So why shouldn't I insist on it for myself?

The shopkeeper who gave me the most respect, and who I had the most respect for, was Martin in Norwich. Martin had so many things on the go at once – running the oldest head shop in the country (founded 1971), refurbishing the oldest house in Norwich (built on the castle ruins), conducting the oldest choir in the oldest church in the city, and being himself the oldest hippy going – that I was impressed. I had been impressed ever since our very first meeting, when Martin had dragged me up to the roof of his shop and shown me all his weed plants.

A little old lady on the opposite roof had shouted over, 'Hey Martin! Have you got any more of that wacky backy?'

Martin had ruffled his mad shock of bushy hair and admitted to me that he supplied all the little old ladies round there. He then emptied my van into the street, stuffed half the contents into a mass of bin liners, gave me a wad of neatly-folded cash, and insisted I smoke some of his special 'home grown' grass. After that, he had taken me down into an ancient crypt in the cellar of his shop, given me a lit candle, and told me to meditate on the silence of the place. Unfortunately, I was so wasted by then I couldn't even hold the candle, let alone 'feel the silence.' But that hadn't mattered. Nor had it mattered when Martin insisted that I make friends with his hyperactive poodle, Muffin. All I had seen was Martin's generous spirit, his spontaneous desire to share all that he had with a virtual stranger.

Muffin wasn't really Martin's poodle; it belonged to his live-in girlfriend, Nikki, but the animal never left Martin's side. And every time I visited, I had to play handball with the highly-strung pooch just to stop it from jumping up and down all over my stock. The only time Muffin actually behaved was when Madge visited with me, and the dog ran off with some of her post-hysterectomy Prozac. Nikki had been furious, but Martin was secretly delighted.

'Have you got any more of those pills?' he whispered. 'I haven't slept so well in years!'

Up until now I had tailored my prices according to how much I liked my customers. It was something I had picked up in India, where the motto was: 'Nice customer, good price. Less nice customer, less good price.'

Martin, who couldn't be nicer, got the best prices of all. But at the end of '98 I stopped giving good prices to anyone. This had nothing to do with the recession, which was nearly over, and everything to do with Sharon, the brassy owner of a shop in Poole. She it was who asked me a question I had never been asked before.

'So Frank, how much profit do you think you make in a year?'

'I don't know,' I said, scratching my head. 'Maybe thirty grand?'

'And how much does it cost you to live in Surrey?'

I hesitated, then admitted, 'I haven't really thought about it. Thirty grand again?'

'So you're living on your "profit"? Where's the profit in that?'

I had no answer for her. All this time, during the long two years since separating from Spud, I had been cutting my prices in order to be the cheapest wholesaler in England. Now my prices were so low that Martin had once coined an epitaph for me: 'Here lies Frank. He was really cheap!'

*

Sharon was right. If I took all my expenses into account—not just the food and household bills, but also the cost of running my van and storing my goods—I was making no profit at all. In fact, I was probably making a loss.

'What kind of mark-up do you charge on your goods?' she persisted.

'It used to be 200 per cent,' I said. 'But it's more like 100 per cent now.'

'That's crazy!' she snorted. 'Whatever I buy from you I mark up at least three times. I couldn't survive otherwise. If you're only doubling up, and your overheads are thirty grand, you've got to sell *sixty* grand worth of stuff each year just to live!'

'Well, thanks,' I mumbled. 'Don't rub it in.'

Having taken stock of my customers, I now had to take stock of my stock. Spud had gone bust for two reasons: half his stock was rubbish, and the other half was too expensive. I had the opposite problem. Most of my stock was good, but because I was charging too little for it, it was worth less than rubbish.

'I think I'll have to retire,' I informed Sharon on our next meeting.

'Oh, you're always saying that!' she jeered. 'Why don't you just put up your prices?'

'I tried that, and nobody liked it. How would you like it if I said you couldn't have a five pound ring tray in your shop anymore? That it would now have to be a ten pound ring tray because I was charging you double?'

Sharon's face fell, then brightened. 'Tell you what,' she suggested. 'Put up your prices for everyone but me, and I'll give you a good idea!'

Sharon's idea was that I stop trading for the whole period leading up to Christmas. All of my shops would be forced to buy elsewhere, she reckoned, and when I resurfaced with my hiked-up prices they would be falling over themselves to pay them.

But when I returned to my shops four months later, half of them didn't want to see me.

'It's not your prices,' explained Pam in Sidcup. 'It's just that you weren't there when I needed you.'

'Where were you before Christmas?' accused Ed in Gosport. 'I rang and rang, and you didn't return my calls!'

Against my will, I was forced to take desperate measures. 'Follow the money,' Spud had once said, so follow the money I did. I brought all my prices back down again and made every effort possible to recover my customer base. If I found a shop with another wholesaler in it, I made sure the other wholesaler was relegated to a back room by offering impossibly big discounts. If a shop lady said, 'I don't want to buy much,' I read her palm, did her horoscope, asked about her family, told her how nice her hair looked, even bought her a Chinese takeaway. Anything to change her mind. I was using all the Indian tactics I'd learned over the years. If all else failed I played the Satish card and gave her 'free' presents.

Elsewhere I spent hours listening to people's problems before I even got to open my van. Topics for discussion might include the health of their cat, the sexual disinterest of their partner, the need to decriminalise cannabis, the best hospital for gynaecological problems, and why everybody should live in tipis not houses.

Finally—and this was a major no-no in the wholesaling world—I started selling to two, even three, shops in the same town. I knew this would force them to compete against each other, using the exact same clothing and jewellery, but I had too much at stake to do otherwise. I had a hundred grand worth of stock in my warehouse, most of it still unpaid for, and I had a lot of strong competition. Spud was out of the frame, yes, but there was a whole load of new wholesalers coming in from India, all of them bombing around the country in big white vans and threatening my livelihood.

I survived. Just. But the next time I saw Sharon, I was not well disposed towards her.

'I didn't think much of your "good idea",' I said. 'It nearly cost me my business!'

'Oh, stop complaining,' she admonished me. 'Have you got any turquoise rings?'

Well, no, I hadn't, but I wasn't saying so. I wanted her to pay for her lousy advice. So I said, 'Malachite is this year's turquoise' and sold her a bagful of cracked malachite instead. Then, when she wanted purple beads (because 'purple went well last time') I stole her glasses and sold her lurid pink instead. Finally, when she rejected the five hundred silk scarves I had specially ordered in for her from India (because 'they're not exactly like my sample') I sold her a pile of base metal toe-rings and called them silver.

'What's all this shit?' she shouted down the phone at me when she finally found her glasses.

'Oh, stop complaining,' I scolded. 'Have you got any more

good ideas?'

₹

Chapter 27

Busy Bobby

Around this time, I got a surprise phone call.

'Hello,' said the voice. 'It's me.'

My heart leapt. _'Spud? Is that really you?'_

'Yes, I've just met a friend of yours. Justin. He thought I might like your number.'

I fought to remain calm. 'Oh, I thought you had it.' I lied. 'How are you?'

'Forget the pleasantries,' Spud said. 'There are some papers in the post. I need you to sign them.'

'What papers?'

'You'll see. And remember, if you _don't_ sign them, I know where you live.'

The phone clicked off, and I began to panic. After three long years, my bald nemesis had found me. I was no longer safe. But when the post arrived the next day, and Spud's letter with it, I was relieved.

'There's some tax due on our old partnership,' Spud had written in his spidery script. 'Just pay the first six instalments with me, and we'll call it quits.'

The six monthly payments totalled £6000, and though the bill had nothing to do with our old partnership and everything to do with Spud's own tax problems, I immediately wrote out six £500 cheques—my half of the deal. It was a small price to pay for Spud's goodwill. Besides, my own recent drug experiences had given me a new sympathy for my brain-addled ex-partner.

'It's my last act of kindness,' I assured Madge. 'He won't bother us again.'

Talk about naïve.

I was also naïve concerning my Buddhist prayer bag. That had been missing for ages, presumed lost. When it turned up again, along with Spud's letter, I took it as a gesture of reconciliation, his method of burying the hatchet. I did a quick check to assure myself that everything was there: my favourite prayer beads, my liturgy book, a few precious photographs, and I thought no more of it.

Really, I should have.

By this time, mid '99, many of Spud's old customers had come over to me, and I was supplying half the country with Indian silver and handicrafts. I did not consider this to be a problem, but apparently it was. In June of that year, I received a letter from the VAT man.

'Dear Mr Kusy,' it read. 'Our records show that you imported £146,000 worth of goods from India during 1998, but you have only declared sales of £49,000 for the same year. Before we send out an inspector, can you please inform us of the location of the outstanding £100,000?'

The outstanding £100,000 was in my pockets—or rather it was in the pockets of people like Satish and Gordhan who had given me unlimited credit. I had only posted sales of £49,000 because that was just below the Value Added Tax threshold, and that saved my customers and me from paying 17.5 per cent extra. To keep my prices even lower—indeed the lowest in the country—I had taken the rest of my sales in invisible cash, failing to declare them to the tax office.

'That's not a very Buddhist thing to do!' Madge scolded.

'I know,' I said with a sigh. 'Karmically speaking, I really must sort out the Inland Revenue in this lifetime.'

'Or?'

'Or I'll probably come back as a beggar on a Delhi sidewalk.'

I was, by my own admission, the worst Buddhist in the world. I smoked, I drank, I told fibs, and I didn't recycle. I was also partial to sausages, despite their well-known impact on greenhouse gases (not to mention my own, as Madge liked to remind me), and I had only the faintest interest in world peace. This was bad, since my brand of Buddhism was all about world peace. But I never stopped thinking I could improve myself, that I could someday abandon my superficial materialism and grow into a more rounded, more mature spiritual being. In the meantime, I consoled myself, while I didn't have much time for the rest of the planet, I did give to those few I felt merited it—to the point of exhaustion.

What I had to decide now was whether the Inland Revenue merited it. I was only planning to dodge tax for a year or two, I told Madge. Just until I had paid off all my creditors and was finally making some profit. But I could hardly tell the VAT this. They would have shut me down without blinking. Instead, I rang my new accountant, Jules, and asked his advice.

'It does look suspicious,' said Jules slowly. 'Where *is* all that outstanding stock?'

'In my warehouse,' I lied. 'They can go see it if they like.'

'Okay,' drawled Jules, sounding somewhat dubious. 'Do you want me to have a word with them?'

'Oh, *could* you?' I asked sweetly. 'You're so very good at

192

this sort of thing!'

After that, I sat by the phone and waited. I had drawn Jules, an immovable force of total dedication, into negotiations with the VAT man, an irresistible object of trained tenacity. My money was on Jules. He was at once the most polite and the most relentless person on the planet. Nobody, to my knowledge, had threatened one of his customers without regretting it.

Sure enough, when the phone rang it was Jules, and he had good news.

'I've just been onto the VAT,' he proclaimed happily, 'and I spent over three hours explaining your situation to them.'

'Well?'

'Well, I don't know what happened,' he admitted, 'but all of a sudden, just as I was about to explain everything for the umpteenth time, I heard this low moan at the other end and they hung up on me.'

I had been lucky. The VAT man never bothered me again. But I'd learnt my lesson. Now that I had nothing left to prove, now that I knew I could make it without Spud, I decided to be sensible and cut back. From now on, I would sell far less stuff to far fewer shops.

The first thing to go was clothing. Yes, the profit margins were huge on the clothes that I sold, but the rest were so riddled with rips, tears, stains, and faulty seams that I had to throw them away. Clothes were also time-consuming – both to make and check in India, and to store and sell in England.

So I decided to farm out all my clothing to big festivals like Glastonbury, and sell only silver to my shops. This semiprecious metal had never been cheaper: only US$5 per troy ounce in 1999, compared to its peak of US$25 back in 1980. And the labour costs of turning it into jewellery in India were minimal. Best of all, unlike clothing, it didn't take up much room and could be transported around England in a few suitcases.

In those days, nobody in India sold more silver than Busy Bobby. Bobby had a three-storey shop at the top of Main Bazar in Delhi, and his ambition was to supply every big wholesaler from the West. To this end, even though he was not much to look at—a pudgy Punjabi with white-powdered skin and a mass of slick black hair—he went out of his way to appear Western. He wore fashionable T-shirts from London, fancy designer watches from Bangkok, and expensive brand name shoes from Rome. He travelled abroad as much as possible, showing at prestigious jewellery fairs, and displayed photos all around his shop of his meetings of important people like Tony Blair and Prince Charles.

But all that came later. When I had first met Bobby, in the spring of '95, he wasn't busy at all. He took me out for meals and to the cinema, and we had a lot of fun together. I liked him for three reasons: he was funny and modest, he had the cheapest silver in India, and he never said 'No.' If asked for something he didn't have, he gazed up at the ceiling and asked, 'Tea? Coffee?' If this failed to distract, he moved onto the subject of food: 'Chow Mein? Chinese fried rice?' If asked a third time, he suddenly remembered a dying relative and vacated the shop.

When I flew into India in May '99, I carried a big sheaf of silver orders and a thick wad of cash—nearly £20,000—to give to Bobby. I knew I was taking a chance, that Bobby was juggling so many customers that he'd started dropping them, but I was gambling that the sheer size of my order, which was over sixty kilos, would compel my busy friend to prioritise me. I was also gambling that paying Bobby up front and in cash would—for once—get my order made on time.

To succeed in my line of work, I reflected, one needed the cunning of a fox, the stoicism of a sacred cow, and the agility of a rooftop monkey. Each buying trip was like a game of Monopoly. You started out with a fixed amount of money to spend, a clear idea of what to buy, and a fairly clear idea of who to buy it from. But then you began to move your piece across the board and the whole neat strategy quickly disintegrated. The dice fell for you, but mainly against you. And for every plus card one drew – like cheap merchandise, good foreign exchange rates, and fun travelling companions – one got a lot more penalty cards, like national strikes, early monsoons, and unforeseen sickness. Somewhere along the line, inevitably, one ran out of money and started playing on credit. And that's when it got tricky – because while Indian traders insisted that 'credit is not a problem', if you didn't pay them back soon, it was a case of 'Go to Pakistan, go directly to Pakistan, and don't come back...ever!'

Having left all my money in Delhi, I travelled on to Pushkar and began living on credit. I didn't want it, I didn't need it, but I couldn't resist it. With two whole weeks to kill before my silver was ready, I was tempted by so many attractive 'buy now, pay later' deals that I started buying clothing again. Once I started, I simply lost track of what was going on. Some orders were being negotiated, others being checked, and still others were being confirmed or cancelled. So many balls were flying around I was dizzy. I wasn't used to buying on my own any more, and with no Spud or Madge around for me to wind down with, my brain filled up with business and went into overload.

I knew I'd reached critical mass when I arranged to meet Satish at 11am and didn't reach him until four hours after that.

I was dealt such a relentless sequence of penalty cards that by the end of the day it was nearly Game Over.

Things started out innocently enough. My 10am breakfast was slightly delayed due to my lemon pancake being cooked on one side only. Then Jagat Singh turned up with an out-of-town Nawab, who wanted me to plug his new hotel in my guidebook. It was no good telling him I wasn't writing any more guidebooks. He wouldn't take 'no' for an answer.

It was gone noon before I escaped the hotel, and as I went I was followed into town by a one-string fiddle player, a guy with a cart, and a trio of desert prostitutes. I tried to walk straight to Satish's but was quickly detoured by a shop offering me the exact same sarongs as Satish had, only three rupees cheaper. Shortly after that, I was lured into a second shop offering me sarongs for two rupees cheaper than shop one. What was going on here? Was Satish ripping me off?

While I was considering this, I was collared by a local *sadhu*, dressed in grubby saffron robes and wearing a small monkey on his head. He led me to a nearby ghat to see 'something special'. This was his friend, sitting by the side of the road selling crocodile oil. Six baby crocs, sweating out tears in the pre-monsoon heat, were crawling around in a small metal basin. And every now and then, the friend was siphoning off the 'crocodile tears' and selling them on as a medicinal cure.

I finally made it to Satish's at 3pm, only to find him 'gone in house.' I rang him there but got his non-English-speaking wife who had no idea who I was. Bored and restless, I went for a shave and emerged with a crick in my neck—the result of an over-enthusiastic head massage. Satish, who had 'just arrive,' took one look at my bare face and shouted 'Ha! *Chickana!*' (fresh-plucked chicken).

Satish and I then held a long and heated discussion over the price of his sarongs. I let myself be convinced that they were worth the extra expense because, as Satish and Sanjay comically demonstrated, they could not be pulled apart by two bull elephants charging in opposite directions.

But I now had a thumping headache, so at 5pm I retired to my room for a sleep. An hour and several aspirins later I returned to the fray, only to find one supplier 'gone to wedding,' a second 'gone to mind children,' and a third 'gone Ajmer.' Frustrated, I decided to spend the rest of the evening with Satish, checking the 1000 sarongs which he was making me on credit.

Then came another problem. Satish had dyed all the material brown. It looked like it had been dipped in cow shit.

'All order cancelled!' I shouted hysterically and stormed outside to cool down.

I returned an hour later to find Satish grinning widely. 'You are lucky man!' he chuckled craftily. 'These things just come!'

And with that he unveiled 1000 metres of sarong material without even a trace of brown in it.

'You are lucky man!' I growled back at him. 'And I think you have these things all the time. Why you show me rubbish first?'

'You are my older brother,' intervened Dinesh dimly. 'Why you no give me calculator as present?'

Feeling my sanity slipping away, I retired to the hotel to stick my head in a bucket of cold water. I had been lied to, shouted at, and generally harangued for twelve hours solid.

Enough was enough. When I phoned Madge in England later on, it was to suggest packing it all in. Travelling alone, without any foreign friends, was far harder than I had anticipated.

'What are you complaining about?' she chided. 'You're approaching the Brechtian ideal!'

'What's that, then?' I asked warily.

'Haven't you heard of Bertolt Brecht? He reckoned that the "ideal man" would be in control of all aspects of his business. And that's you now, isn't it? You're a one-man band, and you do just about everything yourself. You travel to India, you buy all the stuff direct, you check it all out personally, you lug it all home by hand or ship it, you drive it out to your customers in the UK, and you sell it all by yourself and for yourself. Brecht would have loved you!'

'Fair enough,' I said. 'But one question: did Brecht ever go to India?'

*

The following day opened with a famous *sadhu* squatting in the road directly below the Venus restaurant, lifting a 30-kilo slab of granite with his penis. The event drew a crowd of hundreds.

'Ouch, that has got to hurt!' I said, wincing, and pushed my breakfast away.

'What an original way of collecting money!' declared Rose.

Rose was Ram's new girlfriend, and though I had often spotted her knocking around Pushkar, this was the first time I had spent any real time with her. All I knew of her from before was that she had been designing clothes. – first for herself, then for Spud, then for herself again – as a means of getting back to India as often as possible.

Rose was like a past-due-date chocolate: sweet and tempting on the outside, hard as a rock at centre. Pretty and petite, with enormous blue eyes and a Twiggy-like figure, she had a quiet self-assurance which completely belied her fluffy exterior. She inherited this strong inner core, she said, from her high-flying parents—one a banker, the other a barrister—who had always expected her to 'do well for herself'. Having shown an early talent for art and design, she graduated top of her class at one of the better universities.

Then she had come to India and fallen in love with an Indian. Not just any Indian, mind you, but my old friend-turned-fraud, Ram. When I came across Rose that particular morning, she had been writing a letter of complaint about Ram to the management of the Arya Niwas hotel in Jaipur. No sooner had her illicit affair with him emerged than she had been drummed out of the hotel under suspicion of being either a prostitute or a *chubbi-wallah*.

'What's a chubbi-wallah?' I wondered out loud.

She scowled. 'A commission agent. *Chubbi* means twenty-one, and that—in percentage terms—is the amount of commission most Indians pay on sales.'

As she put the finishing touches to her letter, Rose told me—rather tongue-in-cheek— she was planning to get banned from as many hotels in Rajasthan as possible. She was finished at the Arya Niwas, she was *persona non grata* at the Pushkar Palace, and no business hotel in Delhi would touch her because she invited so many men back to her room. The fact that all these men were western buyers who had employed her to check their clothes and silver was immaterial. In India, a single woman being visited by more than one man was obviously a whore.

Rose was now holed up in the Venus restaurant's new hotel. Himmat, the manager, had taken pity on her and given her a private room where Ram could visit whenever he liked. This room had a large fridge in it, containing such western delicacies as Nescafe coffee, Hellmann's mayonnaise, and a super-size pot of Vegemite from Sainsbury's. Most of the fridge, however, was occupied by mangos (this being the mango season), and Rose invited me down to sample a massive bowl of sliced and pulped mangos accompanied by lashings of fresh orange juice. It was the best dessert I had ever tasted.

In the course of our conversation, I learnt Ram had sold shop number one to his brother R.J., and shop number two to his old partner, Yadav. Shop number three had just been opened in his Indian wife's name, this being a crafty court dodge in case Eri, his Japanese ex, decided to sue him for putting her money into shops one and two. Listening to all this made me giddy. If I thought my life was complicated, I needed only to think of Ram's.

Rose wanted me to meet with Ram, but I wasn't too sure. I had never been the forgiving type, and I still remembered the humiliation I had felt when Ram had stood up Madge the year before—not just once, but twice. I also had reservations about the way Ram had betrayed and swindled poor Eri. But on the plus side, and this outweighed everything, I recalled how kind Ram had been to my mother, and how he had helped her to finally understand—and even approve of—my life in India.

So it was with mixed feelings that I turned up at Rose's room that night to make my peace with Ram. The very first thing Ram did, after hobbling forwards for an awkward embrace, was to light up two bidis and hand one to me. It was an old ritual, one that I recognised from long before, and as I accepted it I felt all the anger, all the past bitterness, slip from my heart. Nobody was perfect, I told myself, so why shouldn't I forgive and forget?

Rose was a fine hostess. She flitted busily between us as

Ram tried to explain his behaviour the previous year, and I tried to believe him. He had been unable to welcome Madge, he said, because everyone in Pushkar hated him over the Eri business, and he hadn't felt safe leaving his house.

'Okay,' I said. 'I can accept that. But what about the Eri business? Ten thousand dollars is a lot of money. Don't you feel bad about that?'

'Not really,' replied Ram. 'I intend to pay her back as soon as my shops make a profit.'

I couldn't say anything. Ram's situation exactly mirrored my own with the Inland Revenue. And it was only with the greatest reluctance that I had decided to pay *them* back.

Just then, fortunately, Ram changed the subject. He told me of his four days in jail which, rather than being the nightmare he'd been expecting, had turned into quite a holiday. From the moment he arrived, Ram had felt like a star. Celebrity status had been conferred on him by just one thing: being the first Pushkar person to get his photo on the front page of a national newspaper in twenty years. Everyone had seen his photograph in the *Times of India* and they were all queuing up, in typical Indian fashion, to glimpse the 'famous criminal.' Even the police superintendent of Pushkar jail was in on it. He had prayed that Ram would be sent to his jail and no other, and when this prayer was answered, he told Ram, 'Usually the prisoners I get, I like to see them go quickly. But *you* I hope will stay a long time!'

Ram and I were so happy to be friends again that we decided to celebrate in style. The very next evening saw us enjoying a slap-up meal at the Mansingh Palace in Ajmer. This hotel, we knew, was the only place for miles where we could get away from Pushkar and its ubiquitous vegetables. It was also the last resort for anyone who wanted to remind themselves of what good food and wine tasted like.

We put away a gargantuan meal, running the gamut from mouth-watering chicken *tikka* and lamb *rogan josh* to an 'all-American banana surprise' dessert. Throughout the evening, Ram's eyes kept swivelling towards the classical music trio entertaining the guests—in particular their *tabla* player. He was struck by the uncanny resemblance between the musician and Jagat Singh, manager of the Pushkar Palace hotel. After two or three beers, he was convinced they were in fact one and the same person, and Jagat Singh was leading a double life as a popular entertainer in a four star hotel.

Ram's loud declarations to this effect, coupled with the ensuing hilarity, was disturbed by the arrival of a fat American businessman at our table. He said he was bored by his own dinner guests and wanted to join our party. The inebriated intruder grabbed Ram's left arm by way of introduction, unaware that Ram's arm was hurting from one of his crutches. Ram promptly screamed in pain and told him to fuck off, whereupon the drunken slob slunk back to his own table. Half an hour later he reappeared to touch Ram's foot and beg apology. Ram graciously accepted the apology, since he had now passed his sixth Kingfisher beer and was ready to forgive anybody anything.

It had been good, I reflected later, to spend time again with Ram, good to renew our ties of friendship. But if I thought we were off to a new beginning, I was wrong. As it turned out, this was to be our last supper.

My business in Pushkar completed, I returned to Delhi to collect my silver from Bobby. But first I had to get past Babu.

Babu was a small, fifteen-year-old sex maniac with a penchant for soft-porn western magazines. He knew when I was coming into town, and he knew I always brought him a

'Men Only' from England. I did him this favour because Babu was Bobby's main distraction, even more distracting than Bobby's constant offers of food and drinks. Only a lurid girlie mag could get rid of him.

It took twenty minutes for me to get into the shop. All that time, Babu blocked the doorway, his big brown eyes gleaming in anticipation, his teeth bared in an expectant grin.

'Book?' asked Babu, peering into my bag.

'Not whole book,' I warned. 'One half must go to another man.'

'What other man?'

'Oberoi hotel receptionist. He give me good room!'

'Give me book.'

'No. I can give you one girl only. Which you like, dark or light-hair girl?'

Babu thought carefully, then came back with his verdict.

'*GOOD!*' he said. 'Very *GOOD!*'

And so I had to give him the whole book, with both types of girl in it, which made his huge eyes positively burn with lust. He vanished into the shop toilet, growling as he went, clutching his prize possessively to his chest. He was not seen again for hours.

'We call this boy Bihari Babu,' Bobby said with a low chuckle, 'because he come from Bihar, a very poor place. My father is his uncle and gives him job here so he can send money home to his parents. He is a good worker—except when you bring him book. Then he go crazy!'

Before long, I was going crazy, too.

'It take two weeks, boss!' had been Bobby's response when I placed my order, but I had just given him two weeks and nothing was ready. This was my last day in India, and I had spent most of it sitting in a chair, waiting. Whenever I asked where my silver was, Bobby said simply, 'One man, he is coming in bus from Jaipur.'

I was not alone in his shop. Three other western buyers were sitting with me, miserably supping on their chicken chow meins and anxiously praying that their stuff would arrive before their flights left Delhi airport. As they sat in silent vigil, Bobby made himself as busy as possible, wanting to avoid having to deal with any of us. This brought me to one sad conclusion: Bobby was in business for money only, not friendship.

'I don't want a problem,' I said when I finally cornered him, 'but my plane is leaving in two hours. I can't wait any longer!'

'No problem, boss!' replied Bobby brightly. 'Coffee or tea?'

Minutes later, just as I was about to give up, my silver materialised in a big anonymous sack. With no time to look at it, let alone check it, I was forced to make a quick dash to the airport.

*

As soon as I was back in England, I opened up the silver and gasped in dismay. Half of it was so bad I couldn't even sell it as scrap. Bad stones, wrong designs, faulty workmanship — the list went on. I couldn't even send it back to Bobby because the customs officials at Delhi airport were so corrupt they would simply confiscate the lot.

So I picked up the phone and booked a flight straight back to India. Actually, I booked two flights, since I needed Madge along this time. If we divided the returning silver between us, I calculated, it was less likely to be seized.

Then something quite unexpected happened. The couple from whom we had been renting our house in Surrey suddenly returned from Dubai, and we were forced to find a new home. This was mid-2000, when property values were still quite low, so we quickly pooled our resources and actually bought a house just three doors down from the rental one. It was a good deal, and the only creatures not happy about it were Thomas and Rhetty. I never saw anything so pathetic as those two cats sitting at the top of the stairs, waiting to be dispossessed. They were the last things to be moved out of the old house, and they were the first things to try moving back in. No sooner had the landlords returned from Dubai than they were confronted by two pairs of sad, homesick eyes peering in at them through the garden doors.

I put my flight tickets on hold while we all adjusted to our new lodgings, and made do with the good half of Bobby's silver. It lasted me till just before Christmas, then it was time to hit India again. This time it would have to be more than just India, however. My customers were getting bored with chunky handmade jewellery in the Indian style. Fashions were changing quickly, and the new demand was for lighter, machine-made silver from Thailand, especially chic copies of designer brand names like Nike, Adidas, and Playboy. So I took a gamble and bought an onward flight to Bangkok from Delhi, the plan being to ditch the likes of Bobby forever and buy my silver in Thailand instead.

The second part of the plan was to send Madge back to England on her own with all thirty kilos of Bobby's replacement jewellery, and to save myself lots of freight charges.

It didn't quite work out that way.

₹

Chapter 28

We Are the Agarwals

It was 18ᵗʰ January 2001, and no sooner had we landed at Delhi airport than five customs guys descended on us, pulling handfuls of Bobby's silver out of our bags and shouting 'No allow!'

I explained that it was all reject stuff and had to be returned for exchange, but they wanted to hold onto it. For what reason, I couldn't possibly imagine. It was a Mexican stand-off, and it was only broken when I led the head honcho—a fierce little official with a stiff black hat and a moustache to match—into a nearby urinal and laid two crisp £50 notes on him. After that, he couldn't do enough for us. He even opened the taxi door for Madge and waved us off with a big smile.

Our arrival at the Oberoi Maidens shouldn't have been a problem, but it was. Anil, usually so polite and welcoming, stood at the door with his arms crossed.

'No allow!' he said sternly. 'You are not welcome!'

This was the second time I had heard 'No allow' that day, and my mind raced, seeking an explanation. Whatever it was, it had to be serious.

Before I could ask, he launched into his explanation. 'Your friend, Mister Spud, he bring this hotel into disrepute!'

'Oh,' I said, half-relieved. 'What has he done now?'

'He bring in dirty girls, like prostitute!'

I played back a conversation I'd had with Lou, Spud's ex-wife. She had left him over a prostitute, hadn't she? And since Spud's wealth had never brought him the lusty women he had been expecting, it made sense that he had sought comfort elsewhere.

'I'm sorry about that, Anil,' I apologised, 'but it's nothing to do with me. Spud and I are no longer partners. I mean, we're not even speaking to each other anymore. Look, here are a stack of his bills for people in Delhi, Jaipur, and Pushkar. I must pay these if I want to stay in business. Spud gave me big problem also!'

'You no speak Spud?' said Anil, mildly appeased.

'No, he doesn't!' chipped in Madge. 'Spud want to *kill* him! He try to blow up his house!'

Anil was finally convinced. But as he welcomed us in, all teeth and grins again, he slipped me a piece of paper. It was Spud's unpaid room bill.

Madge wanted to chill out in the Oberoi, since Anil had given us the honeymoon suite, but I wanted to get Bobby's silver back to him. The sooner I returned it, I reasoned, the sooner Bobby could replace it with good stuff. So we dumped our bags in our room and hopped into a waiting hotel taxi.

The driver, a swarthy turbaned Sikh, knew me from before. 'Ha, ha!' he said, laughing. 'Very old man!'

'He means I am a regular customer,' I explained.

'Is that right?' asked Madge mockingly. 'By Indian standards, you could actually be a granddad!'

Outside on the streets, as we headed into town, the poorer elements of Delhi society were fighting an unusually cold January snap by collecting rubber tyres from dead rickshaws or lorries and setting light to them in huge communal bonfires by the side of the road. There was no wood left to burn, so this was the only way they could keep warm, especially in the chilly nights.

Ironically, the air seemed a lot less polluted. Maybe, I mused, the government's drive against diesel was working. The lead-laden smog which always hung over the city was now only a faint haze, and I could actually look around without my eyes streaming and a handkerchief shielding my nose.

Bobby wasn't very happy at having thirty kilos of rubbish silver dumped back in his lap. He had said on the phone that it was 'no problem' returning it, but he obviously hadn't expected us to get it through customs. I came to this conclusion when he explained that the thirty kilos of good silver I'd ordered a month before wasn't available. It was not available because, in Bobby's words, 'One man, he is serious.' This man was so serious, it transpired, that his family had already ordered logs for the funeral fire.

'Is this the same "one man" who forgot to get on a bus from Jaipur last time?' I teased Bobby. 'Because every time I give you an order, there's always a last minute crisis involving "one man." It's like a death sentence, isn't it? I give you an order, you pass it on to "one man", and the next thing I know he's dead, crippled, or afflicted with amnesia!'

At this point, a worried-looking Babu appeared and guided us into the street.

'Who's he?' asked a puzzled Madge, 'and what are we doing out here?'

'It's Babu,' I said, sighing, 'and I don't know.'

We watched Babu go into a weird little pantomime, jumping up and down, flailing his arms about, and burbling

incoherently. All we could get out of him was 'Woman …
downstairs … you know.' Which I eventually translated as
'Give me book, but downstairs, because my uncle is upstairs
and he will confiscate it.'

But I didn't have any books. On this occasion, fearing
Madge's disapproval, I had given the dirty mag racks at
Heathrow Airport a wide berth.

Babu was disbelieving. He was sure I had a book secreted
on me somewhere. 'No book?' he kept repeating, and each
time I said no he looked more cross. When I asked what had
happened to the last one, I learned he had cut it up and sold it
to his mates one girl at a time.

As his anxiety deepened, Babu became more tactile. First
he rooted around in my bag, then he dug his hands into my
pockets, and finally he began running his hands furtively up
and down my trouser legs. In the end, I was forced to call for
assistance. Another few minutes and Babu would have gone
for a full body strip search.

Having left Bobby with strict instructions to have my goods
ready in a week, I hailed a taxi back to the Oberoi. We were
just setting off when a small boy ran up to me and said, 'Hello,
smiling sir! Which country is belonging to you?'

I said, 'What?'

'Which country is currently missing your presence?'

Madge sneered when I gave the boy a tip. 'You're always
tipping people!' she said. 'What for?'

'It's common courtesy,' I replied. 'And anyway, how can
these people live without tips?'

'So the answer is to throw hundred rupee notes all over the
place? I've seen you at the Oberoi: this is for the man on the
door, this is for the guy who polishes the wine pedestal, this is
for the assistant manager's understudy, and this is for the man

who cleans the swimming pool. You're just making it harder for travellers who come after you, don't you realise that?'

I shrugged dismissively, but I soon learnt my lesson. A few hours earlier I had been so pleased at getting my Oberoi breakfast on time that I'd handsomely tipped the room-boy fifty rupees, then promised him another fifty rupees if he brought our evening meal with similar speed. But this didn't happen. Our dinner arrived, cold and burnt, a whole hour after I had ordered it, so I tipped the room-boy only ten rupees. In London, this would have had the effect of restoring normal service, but not here. What I got the following morning was no breakfast at all. Several calls to room service elicited the same bored response: 'Yes sir, coming, coming.' It didn't matter how polite or desperate I sounded, I was obviously being punished for not sustaining the flow of fifty rupee tips.

At 11am, nearly two hours after ordering my food, it finally arrived. 'Happy breakfast!' said the room-boy sarcastically and set before me an inedible Indian *thali*.

'I did not order this!' I complained. 'Where is my bacon, egg, and chips? And why does our coffee pot have no coffee in it?'

'Breakfast time now finish!' declared the boy triumphantly. 'Now is only *thali* possible. So sorry!'

I waved him away and stabbed miserably at an onion. It was the last time, I made a mental note, I would ever give anyone in a hotel a big tip again.

Moments later a loud banging rattled my door. Who could it be, I wondered? An apologetic room-boy come to give me my long-awaited English breakfast? An impatient taxi-driver wanting to take me to Pushkar an hour early? No, it was Satish Agarwal and he was grinning from ear to ear.

'I have found TV!' he announced happily and handed me a

bill.

I had quite forgotten that I had promised Satish this present last time. I had also forgotten that Satish had offered us another lift to Pushkar. I excused myself on the pretext of changing out of my pyjamas, then dug in my room for some cash. While I was gone, Satish and Sanjay invaded the room and polished off the remains of our *thali* breakfasts.

Just as it was time to leave, Sanjay sprang to his feet and said he had to 'go for half an hour.'

'Go *where?*' I asked. 'It's noon and I have to check out!'

But Sanjay was adamant. He had to drive into the centre of town to buy some spare parts for his Maruti van, and he didn't return until 1.30pm. When he did, we all went downstairs and studied the tinfoil Maruti with incredulity. It was hardly big enough to accommodate *us*, let alone Satish, Sanjay, the driver, all our luggage, and Satish's gigantic new TV, which occupied most of the boot. Satish listened patiently to my complaints and then – just a few hundred yards up the road – shoved Sanjay out of the van and stuck him on a bus to Pushkar. Things were a lot easier after that, and I sank back on Madge's lap and went to sleep.

'Ha, *ha!*' declared Satish when I awoke. 'Good *sleeping?*' And then, to Madge: 'You can come to me if you have any marriage problems, because I know this man for six years and I know what make him *tick!*'

'Really?' I asked curiously, raising myself up. 'What's that, then?'

'You are a good man, no problem,' replied Satish. 'Except that sometimes you have an upset mind. When you give me order, I ask you only one thing: please listen why is delay, why is mistake, why is people no working. Then you no upset your mind. If you consider everything slowly, looking at both sides, then you never feeling upset!'

I was not used to Satish having such strong opinions. It was quite a revelation, and the only reason I could see for it was that Satish had been in prolonged contact with Madge, who had strong opinions on just about everything. Satish was so enraptured with Madge that he could—and did—listen to her for hours. It was not what she said that fascinated him so, rather the fact that she was so interested in him. The only other friend of mine he had time for, it turned out, was Gordhan, who was also an Agarwal, and who had some education. Gordhan, I was surprised to learn, was previously a 'government servant'—a teacher just like Madge.

It was fortunate that Satish liked Gordhan, because his Maruti blew a gasket just outside Jaipur, and we had to stay there overnight. That meant a courtesy call to Gordhan, whom we arranged to meet the next day, and a short stop at my old haunt, the Megh Niwas hotel in Bani Park. The Colonel wasn't there, unfortunately, but Indu, his smiley wife, was. She had no rooms, she apologised, but she laid on an 'English tea' on the lawn and let Madge use the heated swimming pool.

Also present was her younger son Ajay, who was now a tall, strapping lad of seventeen with a lazy grin. In temperament, he was very much Indu's boy, sanguine in the extreme and very polite. In physique, however, he bore a striking resemblance to Fateh, or at least to the young Fateh I had seen in a wedding photograph, sitting regally on a horse and wearing a turban. He had the same confident smile, the same shock of wavy black hair, even the same lofty ambitions.

Ajay, we learnt, wanted to be an astronaut. At the very least, he wanted to go to America and study economics. I kept my doubts to myself, but I didn't think sending him to the States was a very good idea. Ajay was altogether too keen, too impressionable, not to be affected by western materialism. God knew what he would come back as—a gum-chewing, glib-tongued yuppie, most like. Whatever happened, his parents weren't going to keep him here much longer. He was bored senseless in Jaipur.

Later on, after putting up at the Arya Niwas hotel, I took Madge to my favourite Indian cinema, the Raj Mandir off M.I. Road. The film we had come to see was *Hum Aapke Hain Koun,* which roughly translated as 'Who Am I To You?' It was apparently the biggest hit in Bollywood history and had not only been running for over a year but had been seen by most Indian families at least five times. Madge and I couldn't make head nor tail of it ourselves, but it was still fun. The film opened at a cricket match, umpired by a perky little dog with a whistle. The hero wore a hat with 'Boy' embroidered on it and was singing joyously into the top of his cricket bat. The heroine wore a T-shirt with the logo 'Bum Chums' and entered stage left on a pair of roller skates, eating two bars of Milky Way chocolate simultaneously. In the next scene she had seamlessly swapped her T-shirt for a new one which said, 'Some Do, Some Don't, and I Might.' The hero, meanwhile, had relocated to an alpine meadow and was singing to a tree. Later on, his loved one burst out of a haystack with a bottle of brandy and embraced a lonely goat.

The film had us both in stitches. We only left halfway through because a rat ran over Madge's foot.

₹

Chapter 29

A "Poor Man's" Castle

The following day, as arranged, we paid a visit to Gordhan's new house.

'My God!' exclaimed Madge. 'It's the size of an airplane hangar!'

I nodded, arms crossed. 'It looks like a pink spaceship, doesn't it?'

'No,' decided Madge authoritatively. 'What we have here is a post-modernist structure along European lines, but with all sorts of other architectural features thrown in. There are traditional Jaipuri elements, of course—the pink brick stonework, the pair of giant bullhorns adorning the entrance— but that giant keyhole in the middle of the façade is pure Dali in its surrealism. And the ogee arch windows are in the late Gothic style. A lot of money has gone into this.' Her eyes were wide with wonder. 'An awful lot of money. I mean, look at the interior: a solid marble floor lounge as big as a football pitch and a ceiling as high as a shopping mall!'

'Not bad,' I said with a snort, 'for a so-called "poor man" who makes no profit!'

A short while later, Gordhan appeared, as fat and welcoming as usual. He was most pleased to meet Madge at last and instantly began force feeding her platefuls of vegetarian food, all the while holding her hand and jabbering away at her in broken English. At one point, unable to contain his jubilation, he turned to me and said, 'She is *much* nice, just like *Mummy!*'

Girish was far more reserved. He now had to get up at 6.30 every morning to go to the gym, a routine he evidently found distasteful. 'It is good for his body,' explained Gordhan. 'He has too much body.' Girish's eyes rolled heavenwards then roamed sceptically across his father's own rotund physique.

Back at our hotel, I asked Madge her verdict on the Jaipur Agarwals.

'Gordhan is a lovely man,' she said. 'A chubby little gnome with grotesque features and an urgent, plaintive voice that's impossible to understand. He really wanted to communicate with me, bless him, but the only words I could make out were "dress quota," something he was obviously upset about. I tried to look sympathetic and nodded my head at what I hoped were the right times, but I can see why he's such a good friend of yours. He's open and honest, with a heart of gold.

'As for Girish,' she continued, frowning slightly as she considered him, 'he looks like a benign young Buddha with a hairpiece.'

'Their relationship is interesting,' I said. 'A year or so ago, I told Gordhan he was lucky to have a son like Girish, a son who spent one hundred per cent of his time building up the business. Gordhan had beamed back at me and said, "Yes! It is better to have one lion than a thousand cubs!" But I don't think he feels that way anymore.'

'Why's that, then?'

'I don't know, but since we last met father and son have gone into some kind of competitive meltdown. They're constantly giving credit to people who never pay them back. First Gordhan lent Spud £25,000 worth of goods, just as Spud was going bankrupt, then Girish stole the show by advancing some Italian $100,000 worth of silver without even asking for a receipt. Both of them are constantly having their house robbed, too, and any profit they do make has to be shared with loads of indolent relatives who don't work at all.'

'The thing that gets me,' added Madge, 'is that they're both so fat. I've always had this idea of strict vegetarians being lean and healthy, but you look at these two and you'd think they've been eating sausages non-stop, with lashings of whipped cream as afters!'

'Vegetarian food in India isn't the same as in England,' I explained. 'It's all cooked in greasy *ghee*—clarified butter— which has more calories than a block of lard. On top of that, Girish smuggles home a pint of ice cream every night, which he gobbles up all by himself.'

Sobered by this conversation, we ordered the healthiest breakfast option possible the next morning: scrambled eggs and fresh mango lassis. Just as we were finishing it, we were summoned by Satish, who finally had his Maruti up and running again. He was keen on getting to Pushkar as soon as possible since he wanted to install his enormous new TV.

*

Three hours later we were settling back into my favourite room, number 111, at the Pushkar Palace Hotel.

'It's all you could wish for when you reach a tropical destination,' said Madge happily. 'Lovely sunny terrace, bright palm trees, and ultra-friendly waiters who make you feel at home. Even the shower works now, so they *have* made an effort!'

Downstairs we were welcomed by a jaunty Jagat Singh, kitted out in pressed khaki trousers, a stylish windcheater, and a pair of reflecting RayBans. What he felt pressed to impart, amongst other things, was his low opinion of beggars.

'When a beggar dies in Bombay,' he said, 'the cops come running, because they know he has lots of money. I have come to know, for instance, that one Indian man who went to Nepal to do business lost all his funds on the bus. He went to the police and they said, "No problem, you just have to go into the street and beg." And that is what he did. And he made enough money to buy his land back, to send his boys to college, and to marry both of his daughters off. He said, "This is my karma— to beg—and it is a lot easier than doing business!"'

Jagat also had a low opinion of Pushkar people, especially puja boys and so-called holy men. 'The other day,' he related, 'a friend of mine said to me, "Jagat, if I had to stay in Pushkar, I would be selling Brahmin barbeques and Sadhu steaks!" And he is correct. These bloody fellows, they are good only for burning! I will never keep a Brahmin in my establishment, and I will never keep his relative!'

The one person of whom Jagat had the lowest opinion was Babloo, proprietor of the adjacent Sunset Cafe. This cafe had originally been the parking space of the Maharajah's elephants, and when Babloo had taken it on he had just— according to Jagat—got out of jail for stealing the starter motor of a Mercedes Benz. Jagat reserved a supernatural amount of vitriol for Babu each day. In his view, Babloo was responsible for every murder, every drug related death, and every arrest of foreign tourists in Pushkar's recent history. If Jagat had his way, Babloo would not just have been hung, drawn, and quartered, but barbecued and tandooried as well.

'Babloo must have a low opinion of me,' I told Jagat, 'for mentioning the rats in his water tank in my guidebook. But he never refers to it. He just leaps to his feet whenever I drop by and grins from ear to ear. I don't know why, but I can't help liking him.'

'You can also like a *dog!*' sniffed Jagat and stormed off.

Speaking of low opinions, everybody in Pushkar, I soon learnt, had a low opinion of me for being over forty and having no children. 'You should take some penicillin!' scolded one shopkeeper, thinking I must have some rare disease since I was so old and still childless. 'You must do your *duty!*'

'That's nothing!' snorted Madge. 'I didn't tell you earlier, but Satish had a word with me back in the van. He asked whether I had any children, and when I said no, he laughed and said, "Ha, ha! You must be *grandmother!* Because in India, at the age of forty, you must be a grandmother!" I explained to him that children were out of the question, that I had a medical problem, but he was not to be deterred. He went on and on about these healers I could try, a magic bracelet I could wear, and how I should go down to the lake and do some special puja to the gods. The idea that we could never have kids was totally unthinkable to him, because he wanted us to be the "same same" as him, and this was not possible when he had children and we didn't.'

Speaking of Satish's children, we met them when we made the obligatory trip to his house. He had two boys and a girl, and all three were beautiful. They were dressed to the nines—the boys in little sailor suits, the girl in a fetching little smock—and they all had big brown eyes, painted around with black kohl. Shy and well-mannered, they only broke ranks and rushed forward when I produced a pack of western chewing gum.

As for the house, it was a complete contrast to Gordhan's. The building was a crumbling, ramshackle affair secreted in the bowels of Pushkar's back streets. The only approach was via a narrow, potholed lane down which Sanjay, on his motorbike, drove us at high speed.

When we arrived, we stepped into a small courtyard smeared with animal dung and dotted with wads of dead chewing gum. To the right of the courtyard was an underground concrete bunker, where Satish's twenty or so subterranean tailors were secretly stitching up clothing. 'Here is safe, no problem with duplicators!' he told me.

On the other side was Satish's house, dark and dim at street level but painted a wild pink upstairs, the ceiling adorned by long lines of laundry. Behind these was the 'business lounge' which offered a small table and two cheesy-green sofas. Looming over the back sofa was the new 42-inch screen TV, playing loud Hindi movies. Next to the TV stood a high, velvet-covered shelf, occupied by a gently snoring relative who was 'just visiting'. The only other room we saw upstairs was the kitchen, where the ladies of the house were constantly cooking. Satish and his brothers darted in and out at regular intervals, both to sample the results and to force feed us foreign guests because we were 'too thin.' Satish was particularly keen that we partook of anything cooked by his mother, whom he regarded with a level of respect bordering on awe.

The two Agarwals Madge liked best, she confided later, were Satish and Gordhan. They both had the same childlike simplicity, the same eagerness to please, and the same willingness to laugh at anything, even if it was at their own expense. At first she had been shocked at my rudeness to them, making comments like 'What's this rubbish? Take it away!'

but then she'd realised it was all part of a game – that when I got *very* upset, they just gave me a big smile and asked, 'Take some chai?' And that when I cracked up at this absurdity, they were so relieved they ran over to embrace me, saying, 'Oh, funny man, funny man!'

It wasn't through ill-will or incompetence that they produced badly fitting clothes, Madge chided me. It was just that they were making stuff they simply didn't *wear*.

'Take Satish for instance,' she said. 'It's taken you years to train him up to make western-style hippy dresses and skirts. Up until he met you, all he knew how to make were Rajasthani kurtas, saree-suits, and woollen ponchos. He must have ditched hundreds of samples before he got it right, so you've got to admire his stamina!'

This was the one thing that bothered me about Madge in India. Even after she knew it was just a game, that I only savaged traders who totally deserved it, then laughingly forgave them, she kept leaping to the defence of people like Satish, who had, as it happened, just got something wrong again.

'It wasn't his fault,' she complained stubbornly. 'He did his best, so it must have been down to you. You couldn't have explained it to him properly!'

I knew better than to disagree. If I knew one thing by now, it was that Madge had a simple, almost naïve sympathy for anyone for whom she felt sorry, and when it came to 'poor' Indians she would defend them to the death. It didn't matter how badly or how often they screwed things up. In her opinion—and it was a maddening opinion that made me want to bang her head against the wall—"You *must* treat these people with respect, not like ex-Raj colonial subjects!"

₹

Chapter 30

Mister Duplicator

I knew I was sick when I lost it in the market.

There was an irritating band of oily characters on the fringes of Pushkar society who made it their job to hassle travellers. 'Remember me?' they'd croon, and before one had time to say no, they would follow up with the demand 'Where is my gift?'

This particular day, it got too much. One guy sidled up to say 'Forget *me*?' and I just snapped.

'Forget you?' I snarled. 'I'd *love* to forget you. Just tell me how! If I could forget you, I would die a happy man!'

Madge swiftly guided me back to the hotel and put me to bed. I wasn't safe on the streets, she decided, and neither was anyone else.

It was not I who ended up in hospital, however, but Madge. Minutes after taking my temperature and finding it to be a ripe 104, she discovered a horsefly inside her mosquito net and broke her little toe while trying to stomp it against the wall.

I watched in semi-delirium as a white VW van drew up—Pushkar's answer to an emergency ambulance—and carried Madge away. An hour passed, then another. Satish turned up with some fabric samples which I listlessly checked. A couple more hours went by, with my slipping in and out of consciousness, before the door to our room burst open and Madge hopped toward me on one foot, looking totally outraged.

'You won't believe this,' she spluttered, 'but I've just been *abducted!* I was the only passenger in that van, and the driver was mad—quite mad. He didn't speak a word of English, and he kept frightening people off the road with his stupid siren. He drove me out to the middle of the desert and set me down at this gigantic airline hanger which turned out to be a 'hospital.' I was left for hours in a dark concrete bunker with no chairs and lots of sick people moaning on the floor until someone finally appeared with a wheelchair. I was cranked into a vast hall occupied by one x-ray machine, and I only stopped screaming when I saw the word Siemens on it. That's when I realised they were only going to scan me, not torture me. Turns out I hadn't broken the toe, thank God, just sprained it, but I tell you one thing. You don't want to fall ill in India, *no way!'*

Three days later, with both of us more or less recovered, we were on our way back to Delhi in the Maruti van. If all went well, Madge would soon board a plane back to England carrying a bagful of Bobby's silver, and I would fly on to Bangkok for a quick three-day jewellery buy. We were in an optimistic mood.

Halfway to Jaipur, Madge leant towards Sanjay Ajarwal, who was sitting up front with the driver. 'What shall we bring you next time as a present?' she asked. 'A T-shirt with "I Love London" on it?'

Well, Sanjay positively sneered at this suggestion. His idea of a present was nothing less than a zoom-lens Kodak camera or a state-of-the-art Gameboy with lots of buttons. He didn't say as much, but the sneer, coupled with the phrase 'Bring what you like,' told us exactly what he thought of the T-shirt idea. He then informed us he could make anything that Gordhan manufactured, and for half the price—though he said he was not out to ruin Gordhan. He did have his scruples.

'Why you not make me Gordhan-style dungarees?' I asked. 'I give you sample one year before. You lose it?'

'I no lose,' declared Sanjay confidently. 'I am Mister Duplicator. I copy everything quick and easy. But Gordhan no happy I make dungarees, so I no make. He has little business, so he is happy. I take his business, he is crying. He is Agarwal, he is relation, so no good I make him unhappy.'

Speaking of Gordhan, we dropped in on him in Jaipur. He was as jolly as ever and just as incoherent. I got a great photo of him, again explaining the intricacies of black-market quotas to Madge. His face was screwed up with agitation, his brow furrowed in an expression of pain while Madge stared back at him, wearing a forced smile of polite interest. As before, she didn't have the faintest idea of what he was talking about.

Back on the road, we found out what Sanjay did want as a 'present.' He wanted to come to England and buy a fridge. Ever since the January before, when the Indian government had floated the rupee against other international currencies, the black market in foreign exchange had vanished. Indians could now travel to England and the States with as much foreign currency as they liked. They didn't need to buy it 'on the black' anymore, and were thus making frequent trips abroad to kit their homes out with the latest hi-tech domestic appliances—including fridges. The rupee had now devalued to 65 to £1—a 20 per cent decrease—but that didn't put them off in the slightest. In India, you were what you owned, and they were prepared to pay for it.

'Despite this,' said Sanjay, 'money is very tight in India.'

He didn't know why, but he had noticed that very few buyers were coming to India. Of the twenty-seven foreign wholesalers who had crowded out the Venus restaurant just three years before, the only survivors—according to Sanjay—were me and American George. Pushkar had had its day in the sun, a brief decade of glory, and now it was almost over. The recent recession had a lot to do with it, I theorised, though it was probably just as much to do with people like Ivan and Spud, who had sold tons of damaged silk to shops and spoilt it for everyone.

The Maruti screeched to a halt around 7pm, just as Bobby's shop in Paharganj was closing. Somehow my thirty kilos of replacement jewellery had made a showing, and we managed to cram it into Madge's already jam-packed luggage. We then raced to the airport by taxi, and I ushered Madge onto the plane. Problem over, I thought.

Of course not. It was just beginning.

A casual glance at my own ticket sent sweat immediately to my brow. It wasn't my ticket at all. My name was now Madge, and I was going to London. This meant Madge was now me, and she was on her way to Bangkok. Somehow, in all the rush, the tickets had got mixed up. My only recourse was to dash up the tarmac to her plane—its turbines already gunning and ready for take-off—and rummage through her handbag while the other astonished passengers watched me exchange the tickets and dash back off again. Madge was completely unaware. She was in the toilet and missed the whole thing.

Throughout this feverish activity, one question burned in my brain: how on earth had she been allowed on the wrong plane in the first place?

It was an ominous start to an ill-fated side trip.

₹

Chapter 31

Thai-Tracked

'What is *this?*' demanded Mr Missal, pulling handfuls of
silver jewellery out of Madge's luggage. 'Why you no declare
this?'

Madge had arrived at Heathrow airport after a long night
flight from Delhi and wandered into the 'goods to declare'
channel with only one thought in mind: 'Will I be in time for
my first morning class?' The fact that she might have a
problem with Bobby's silver hadn't occurred to her. It hadn't
occurred to me, either. As far as I was concerned, it was a
straight swap of good for bad goods, and I had already paid
duty on the bad stuff, so why should I pay it again?

Mr Missal was the duty customs officer at red channel that
day, and he couldn't believe his luck. Here was an obvious
criminal trying to smuggle goods past his nose with not even a
receipt to justify their presence.

Tony, my import agent, looked at Madge in bewilderment
as if to say, 'What have you *done?* How can I possibly *help*
you?

'I don't know what you're talking about,' Madge muttered
wearily. 'My husband told me to bring it through, and he said
it was okay.'

'Oh,' sniffed Mr Missal, 'and I suppose if he told you to bring through thirty kilos of *drugs*, that would be okay, too?'

At this point, Madge's earlier stoicism, the result of twenty hours of no sleep, gave way to outraged indignation. 'Look here, you self-important little man!' she snarled. 'Are you trying to imply I'm an international drugs smuggler?'

Mr Missal wasn't used to being talked at this way. He was a small, arrogant Indian, used to meek pleading and profuse apology from 'criminals' he had caught. He was supposed to humiliate them, not them him. Without a further word, he frog-marched Madge into a dark interrogation cell with a chair chained to a table, and shone a bright beam in her face for further questioning. Madge was not pleased. Instead of breaking down and crying, as he expected her to do, she went cold and hostile on him, winding Mr Missal up even further and guaranteeing her an extended stay in that manacled chair.

'How many times have I got to say it?' she shouted at last. 'I don't know what I've done wrong. I am *not* a criminal, and I've got thirty students waiting for me in a classroom. If you don't let me out of here right now, I am going to *scream!*'

Mr Missal briefly considered chaining her to the wall for his own protection, then thought better of it. Here was a kind of criminal he had not come across before: a totally unrepentant and volatile one, and he took two steps back before issuing his next and last volley.

'Why are you so *upset?*' he demanded. 'What do you have to *hide?*'

I wouldn't have wanted to be there to see the flash in Madge's eyes. I've seen it before. 'Don't raise your voice to *me,*' Madge advised imperiously, 'or I'm going to file a complaint about you bullying people! I want to see your superior *right n*ow!'

With that she made a vicious lunge for him, forcing him to scuttle out of the cell and double-lock the door behind him.

Half an hour later, his 'superior' arrived. He was a tall, avuncular figure with much better people skills, and he managed to calm Madge down. After just a few short questions, he decided she was innocent and let her go. But although she did make her class (just about), she had not forgotten *my* part in all this. I had nearly cost her her job, she reasoned. She had been rudely (and unfairly) abused by a jumped-up little official and had nearly acquired a criminal record. And she was not going to forgive me that for a very long time.

Neither was Mr Missal. His dignity had been seriously affronted by his encounter with Madge, and he was in the mood for revenge. He may have been forced to let one criminal go, but there was still one left in the bag. He had all my flight details, and he had all my silver. And he waited, oh so patiently, for me to fly in from Bangkok and lay claim to it.

Blissfully unaware of all the high drama going on back home, I proceeded into Thailand to buy yet more silver, thereby compounding my problems tenfold. Little did I know it, but I was about to make Mr Missal's day—perhaps his year.

*

I had been to Bangkok many times before, researching my guidebooks on Thailand and Southeast Asia, but I'd never been there for business. Spud had been there on his own back in '93, but that had been a disaster. He had hit Chinese New Year, not just in Thailand but in Vietnam as well, and all the shops had been closed for a week.

It was now 27th January, and if my calculations were

correct, I had three days to get all my buying done before the same thing happened to me. In my haste, however, I made a fundamental mistake. Instead of resting up in a hotel, as any sensible person would have done, I shrugged off jet-lag and went on a manic shopping spree straight off the plane. Ten hours later, and clutching two big bags of silver in my hands, I fell asleep in the back of a taxi ... and woke up in Cambodia.

The first I knew of this was the driver announcing, 'Hotel, boss!' followed by a posse of Cambodian border officials asking for my passport. The cabbie hadn't understood my slurred instructions, and instead of taking me to the Amari Boulevard, my hotel of choice, he had driven me all the way up Sukhumvit Road—the longest road in Asia—to a completely different Amari in a completely different country. Before the curious Cambodians got wind of the twenty kilos of brand new silver in the boot, I grabbed the wheel, made the driver turn round, and sent us spinning four hours back to Bangkok. It was a close call.

The trouble with shopping in Bangkok, and the reason I had been unable to stop, was that the Thai silver was so *good*. Not only was the quality much finer than in India, since it was machine made, but it was also well tuned into the current fashions in world jewellery. Bangkok was the copy capital of Asia, and amongst other things it was now turning out the latest trend in ultra-violet and body jewellery, which was all the rage in the West.

Bangkok was also, in my opinion, the Las Vegas of the western wholesaler: a whole new game with lots more chips with which to play. Though for every buyer who bet well and made money, I guessed, there would surely be others who bought too much of the wrong thing, and at the wrong time, to ever be able to afford to come back again. Not only were the stakes much higher, but the practiced, painted smile of the Thai trader—so much like a Vegas Baccarat croupier—tempted one to play on and on until, quite suddenly, it was Game Over.

I didn't want to use my credit card, but somehow it just kept popping up. The English pound was so strong and the silver so cheap, that I had to mentally slap myself every so often to stop going overboard. I had begun following Argentinians and Italians around silver shops since they seemed to have the best idea of what was 'in' and fashionable. What they bought in tens, I bought in hundreds. The buying buzz was truly upon me, and by the end of my second day I was still awake at 4am, ploughing through my treasure and trying to price it all up.

It wasn't just a matter of making money. To me it was more to do with finding something new and exciting to show my customers back home, the anticipation of saying, "There you go. Check *this* out!" There was nothing in my mind like showing a whole load of new lines to jaded customers who had got in the habit of rolling their eyes and asking, "Same old shit again?" At the same time, however, I knew I had to put a brake on my spending soon. I had gone through £14,000 already, and it would take me months to claw it all back.

Maybe it was the novelty, but I found Thailand surprisingly easy to deal with after India. The smog of diesel hanging over Bangkok was even worse than in Delhi—so dense indeed that saffron-robed monks emerged from it coughing into their begging bowls—but the city was otherwise quite tourist-friendly.

The shops were easy too, relaxed and honest. And unlike India, they could attend to me without a constant series of interruptions from telephone calls, sadhus passing by for alms, vagrant cows nibbling at clothing, and unhygienic Pepsi bottles being handed over. Most Thai shops, I was even more surprised to find, were pleasantly air-conditioned and all the jewellery was stacked in transparent little boxes. Each one was labelled and coded so the buyer could see at a glance what was available and what wasn't. One final bonus: there was no end to the shopping experience. The Thais lived even more on the job than the Indians, kicking off work around 10am and closing as late as midnight.

After the last day's shopping in Ko-Sahn, however, I was back in my room considering a problem.

I had too much luggage. I'd stupidly brought twenty-five kilos of Pema goods in from Delhi, and now I had mountains of silver to pile on top. At this point I realised how mad I had been to do India and Thailand together. The luggage from even one of these countries was enough to give me trouble at airport check-in, let alone two.

In my head, alarm bells began ringing. Even the most careful packing left me with two thirty kilo suitcases—one for the main hold of the plane, one for hand-carry—plus a fifteen kilo shoulder bag, which I hoped nobody would notice. The sheer scale of my over shopping became apparent when the bellboy came to collect my bags. He bent down to pick them up ... and his arms remained rooted to the floor.

'Wow!' he muttered respectfully and rang for a trolley.

The two big bags actually weighed in at thirty-five kilos each. I found this out at Don Muang airport, where—totally against expectations—all my luggage was checked through with a big smile.

'Today is *lucky* day!' the ground hostess informed me. 'Chinese New Year, so empty flight!'

It was so empty I was offered a triple row of seats in which to sleep during the twelve hour flight to London.

But that was as far as my luck went. I wandered off the plane at Heathrow, feeling pleased with myself, and strolled straight into the arms of Mr Missal.

'Ah, Mr Kusy,' purred Madge's old adversary. '*There* you are!'

I glanced around the customs hall and determined I was the only person present—except for Tony, my agent, who squirmed uncomfortably in a corner. Tony knew what was coming, and one look at his terrified eyes spoke volumes. I was in deep, deep trouble.

Mr Missal didn't bother asking if I had anything to declare. He just ushered me into the interrogation cell, the same one in which Madge had languished, then he left me in the manacled chair to consider my fate. When he returned, a long hour later, his face was creased in a triumphant smirk, and his thick brush moustache simply twitched with excitement.

'Do you know what you are, Mr Kusy?' he asked, practically tittering with anticipation. 'You are a *crim-in-al!*'

'No, I'm not,' I protested. 'I have receipts for everything!'

'Yes, yes,' said Mr Missal indulgently. 'Very low value receipts which cover only *half* the jewellery you bring in. Then there is matter of the Indian silver, the thirty kilos which you ask your wife to smuggle through. They have no receipts at all.'

'I didn't ask her to smuggle anything!' I said hotly. 'That stuff didn't need receipts. I'd already *paid* duty on it before I exchanged it back in India!'

'And you didn't think to apply for a re-importation certificate? Your agent did not tell you this?'

Well, no, I hadn't. I hadn't said anything, because I hadn't thought to tell him what I was planning to do. It was, as they

say, a fair cop. I had no option but to hold up my hands and let
Mr Missal do his worst—which was very bad indeed. With a
hungry grin he confiscated half my Thai silver, and all of
Bobby's silver, then fined me £2000 for importing counterfeit
Nike and other brand name jewellery. To top it all off, he put a
black mark on my name, so that whenever I flew in from Asia
again, Mr Missal would be there in person to be my very own
judge and jury. In the background, I heard Tony groan at the
tough sentence.

All this, however, was nothing compared to my reception
back home. As soon as I turned the key to my front door, I was
confronted by all seven furies rolled into one: an aggrieved,
red-faced Madge in full Doberman attack mode. She
proceeded to give me such a tongue-lashing I felt whipped
raw. She had been grilled for two hours by Mr Missal, she had
never been so humiliated in her life, she had almost lost her
job and gone to jail, and it was *all my fault!*

I waited, stunned, until she finally ran out of steam. Then I
watched her stomp up the stairs, gathering up two mildly
protesting cats as she went, and barricade herself in the master
bedroom. At the bottom of the stairs was a note. Its message
was short and sweet. 'Thank you for nearly destroying my
life,' it read. 'Don't involve me with your stupid business ever
again. Go away and stay away. Furiously, Madge.'

That didn't leave much room for negotiation, but I had to
try anyway. I attempted to explain myself through the locked
door, but that didn't work. Then I slipped a piece of chicken
roll under the door, hoping to provoke a fight between the cats,
but that didn't work either. All that achieved was two airborne
pussies chucked in my face and the door slammed back shut
again. The only thing that did work, after hours of persuasion,
was the promise of a five star holiday to the destination of her

choice. Even then, it took weeks to calm her down properly and for me to 'learn my lesson'.

In the meantime, I was facing total ruin. With three-quarters of my silver confiscated and my credit card spent to the max, I was seriously considering bankruptcy. I phoned American George for advice and was told, 'You've got some stuff left, haven't you? Just triple your prices, man! That's what I would do!' But I couldn't do that. I couldn't punish my customers for what was, after all, my own stupid mistake. So I did the only other thing left to me. I sold all that I had in quick order, and bet everything on one final roll of the dice: one last trip to Asia. This time, I promised myself, I would be a good boy and play by the rules. If I fell into the hands of Mr Missal again, I would give him no reason, not even the tiniest missing receipt, to punish me.

But fate is a fickle thing. As it turned out, I gave Mr Missal so much ammunition, he could have had me locked up for years.

₹

Chapter 32

A Very Bad Year

There comes a point in every wholesaler's life when he feels like throwing in the towel, when he thinks to himself: 'It's been a good game, I've had a fun run, but now it's time to check out.'

2001 was a bad year for me. A very bad year. Just as I was licking my wounds from Mr Missal, just as I was getting ready to travel again and recoup my losses, I received a letter from the Inland Revenue. It contained a bill for £40,000. The bill belonged to Spud, who had somehow managed to transfer his own business failure to my account. As a final act of retribution for me 'deserting' him three years before, he had managed to convince the IRS that I was still his partner when he went bankrupt, and I was therefore liable for all his debts. This worked—despite the fact that we had never had a written partnership agreement, and I had set up my own company months before Spud went down the drain.

I was fed up with paying Spud's bills. I had already paid off his staff, most of his suppliers in India, even his solicitor and his accountant. I was blowed if I was going to pay Spud's whopping tax bill as well. But what else could I do? Spud had cleverly sealed my fate (back in '98) by tricking me into paying the first six instalments of his bill, then paying nothing himself. The whole bill automatically became mine, and I had a feeling the reek of this particular stink bomb would not go away for many, many years.

*

Then, tipped off by Spud, the Inland Revenue slapped a court order on my house in a final attempt to reclaim their forty grand, and threatened to repossess it if I didn't pay up.

I made a desperate call to Jules. 'Look,' I said, 'I know you're my accountant, not my solicitor, but what would you do to get out of this mess? I'm about to end up on the street!'

There was a long pause at the other end of the phone—so long that I thought he had been cut off—then George asked,

'How is your health?'

I blinked. 'What do you mean?'

'Well, as far as I know, they can't do you if you're sick.'

'How sick?'

'Very sick.'

I gave a pained smirk. I *was* very sick. I just hoped somebody would believe me.

Four days later Jules's wife—who was a solicitor and who did believe me—rolled me into the main office of the Inland Revenue in a wheelchair. I hadn't slept in three days and was a helpless, gurgling wreck.

'How dare you threaten my client in this condition?' she berated the tax officer, but he was unmoved. I had sixty days to pay up, he informed her, or the bailiffs would move in.

Spud. Wherever I went, whatever I did, Spud was determined to destroy me. Trying to blow up my first house was one thing. Telling the taxman my new address so they could seize the second was quite another. What other schemes might this little maniac have in store?

Thrashing about in my bed, driven half-crazy by growing paranoia, I began taking Valiums on a nightly basis.

*

Madge was not amused by this situation. Not amused at all.

'You've got 60 days before we lose the house?' she screeched hysterically. 'Well, I'm not paying that bill – it's your mess!'

'Not really,' I countered. 'I got tricked into it.'

'I told you not to trust that bald little thug. Only an idiot would have believed him! Oh, and what happened to the self-professed cool dude I fell in love with? Drugged up to the eyeballs with sleeping tablets, you're turning into a zombie!'

Drastic measures were called for.

I don't know what came over me, I hated to think what would happen if Madge ever found out, but I rang up a psychiatrist, showed him my most recent hair transplant scar, and said, 'I'm not safe on the streets. Look, I just picked a fight with the missus and she banged me round the back of the head with a bottle!'

He got me admitted to hospital in a flash.

*

Let no-one tell you that a drug rehab unit is a picnic. It isn't. The moment I got in, I thought 'Oh God, what have I done?' A dozen or so shadowy figures surveyed me suspiciously from the dark, dimly lit communal recreation area. All of them wearing dressing gowns, all of them smoking cigarettes.

'Oi, mate!' called out one of them. 'What you in for?'

'Sedatives,' I replied, and they all laughed.

That was when I realised I was in the wrong place. This wasn't a nice, cosy holiday camp for Valium sufferers. It was in fact a hard-line smack ward, full of recovering heroin addicts. And the funny thing was, I knew half of them. They'd come from the methadone clinic down the bottom of my road, and I'd been giving them money for years.

'Ere, I know you,' said one guy menacingly. 'You're a copper, aren't you?'

'No, I'm not,' I replied. 'Why? Do I look like one?'

'Yes, you do,' he said. 'If you're not a copper, prove it!'

His way of 'proving it' was to stick my head in a bucket and shave it. Which turned out to be a good thing.

'Fuckin' hell!' he pronounced as my gruesome hair transplant scar came into view.

'Where did you get that?'

'Oh, the wife bottled me,' I replied casually. 'Does it look bad, then?'

'It looks fuckin' awesome!' he exclaimed. 'That's what I *call* a scar!'

Everyone gathered to touch and finger the back of my head, and Mister Menacing clutched me to his chest like a long lost brother.

'My name's Steve,' he whispered confidentially. 'Anything you want in here, just ask for me.'

*

Nights were the worst. That's when the communal dormitory turned into a living hell of snoring, hallucinating, screaming psychos. They'd been issued their daily ration of methadone earlier in the day, and it hadn't been enough. I jammed my earplugs in, to drown out their nightmares, but I couldn't sleep. My body, pumped up with enough sedatives each night to tranquillise a full-grown pony, was suddenly very much awake.

I lay a prisoner in my bed for hours, and when I did finally drop off, I woke up to find a razor at my throat.

'If you snore one more time,' said a ghostly voice, 'I'm going to slit your throat.'

Well, that did it. I didn't sleep at all after that.

On the fifth night, I finally broke down. I'd held myself together up till then with constant chanting – hours of it, in the dining room, the shower, even the toilet. The staff got so pissed off with me – especially when Steve and his croniessigned up and it became a general pray-in – that they 'forgot' to give me my medication. Result? I went into rapid cold turkey withdrawal and was found, that awful fifth night, a crying, hysterical wreck on the carpet.

They quickly gave me something to calm me down, but the damage was done. I would never sleep well again.

*

Madge welcomed me home with mixed feelings. On the one hand, I had been in that place just long enough (two weeks) to qualify as a bona fide recovering addict – the taxman tore up the court order and the bill bounced straight back to Spud. On the other, I had returned to her in a lot worse condition than I had gone in.

'Are you sure you want to go back to work again?' she said, concerned.

'It's not a matter of wanting to,' I gurgled unhappily from my sick-bed. 'It's a matter of *having* to.'

₹

Chapter 33

On being a Bad Buddhist

It was a Friday night that I got nicked.

My mobile rang, and it was Spud. 'Check your glove compartment,' he said mysteriously, then he was gone.

I was in the van, driving home from Sidcup, and nearly lost the wheel.

Reaching into the glove compartment, I discovered a pack of ecstasy pills and promptly did lose the wheel. I plunged off the pavement and into some old lady's rose garden. To top it all off, a police squad car materialised out of nowhere and arrested me. 'Driving in possession of Class A narcotics,' they cautioned me as they wrestled the pills out of my sweaty fist. They left the van where it was, with the old lady still hopping around on her decimated roses, and drove me down to Bexleyheath police station.

I was well acquainted with this police station. It was situated exactly where my old bedsit had been five years before, so it almost felt like coming home. I even suggested that I might have the cell where my old room had been, but that only earned me an 'Are you taking the piss?' and a thump across the shoulder.

Spud had obviously set me up by ringing the police and

leaving an anonymous tip. But I couldn't prove it. They had me bang to rights, and I was looking at a nasty little jail sentence. Possibly even a nasty big jail sentence, since there were eleven pills in that packet. Anything over ten meant I was 'dealing' rather than casual using.

What saved me was all the crap in my pockets: all the business cards, tat souvenirs, diesel receipts, fag butts, congealed sweets, and assorted loose change gathered down the course of the years.

'How many pockets have you *got?*' asked the policeman, itemizing all my loot. He was scowling, trying to detach a wad of dead gum from a faded holographic picture of Krishna.

'Nineteen,' I said brightly.

He groaned and told me to go home.

*

I flew into Bangkok at the end of September 2001. My right buttock was paralysed from tromping through the mud at Glastonbury, followed by six weeks on the road selling in England and Wales. All that lifting and bending over the course of the past ten years was finally getting to me. I didn't know how long I could keep it up, even whether I should be keeping it up. My whole back was a mass of accumulated scar tissue, and unless I learnt to slow down and look after myself, my days as a travelling salesman could soon be over.

I limped off the plane looking like John Wayne, lurching forwards from my hips with my jaws tightly clenched. They had given me an orthopaedic chair on the plane to help me sleep, but this had provided only temporary relief. By the time I reached the Amari hotel in Sukhumvit, I was a cripple once more.

Fortunately, funds being low, I was only in Thailand for three days. Even more fortunately, I found everything I needed in one shop, barely two hours after touchdown. The shop was located in the Narayana Phand complex, opposite the World Trade Centre, and it was owned by a fat, smiley lady named Anne. She had all the copy Nike, Adidas, and Playboy earrings which Mr Missal had earlier confiscated, together with matching rings, pendants, and bracelets. No, I wasn't being stupid when I bought them again. I had a plan. The plan was to take all this counterfeit stuff to India and send it home from there, mixed in with Bobby's jewellery.

Good plan. Sort of.

The only thing Anne did not have, and that went for all the Thai shops, was any good stones, either precious or semi-precious. I would have to go back to India for those. I knew by now that to get a good cross-section of jewellery, both plain silver and silver with stones, I would have to travel straight from Bangkok to Delhi.

I returned to the Amari around noon, practically paralysed with pain. The final blow to my back had been brought on by a horrifically dangerous *tuk-tuk* ride. Tuk-tuks are the most common mode of transport in Bangkok. They are also the most hazardous. They resemble the auto-rickshaws of India, but have a lot more zip—and a lot less regard for the law. My driver, totally ignoring my howls of pain, sped me home via five hotel car parks, two shopping malls, and more private forecourts and backstreets than I thought possible. In Bangkok, I thought, one didn't buy a ride. One bought a lottery ticket.

With no other choice, I called the hotel doctor: a fat, confident individual named Dr Ratt, who promptly came upstairs and gave me a shot in the bum. Minutes later my central nervous system shut down, and I couldn't move off the bed. Then, for some reason I will never understand, Dr Ratt began stuffing me full of bananas. A large plate of bananas sat in my room, and the doctor made me eat every one of them.

Just before Dr Ratt left, a bellboy appeared with a fresh bowl of fruit. This was quickly shoved down my throat as well. I felt like a malnourished monkey being force-fed an orchard. The bowl contained a lot of one particular fruit I had never seen before, and when I asked what it was I was told, 'These are sort of cantaloupes. Very good for you!' Moments before falling asleep, I spotted a large cockroach perched on the single remaining cantaloupe. It was welcome to it.

The following morning, to my great relief, the pain was almost gone. The good doctor's injection seemed to have worked. I abandoned all thoughts of going home in a wheelchair and headed out shopping again.

September appeared to be a good time to visit Thailand. The shops were full of new stock, since there were a lot of other wholesalers around, and though it was supposed to be the end of the rainy season the weather was surprisingly dry and cool. By contrast, I couldn't help thinking, it hadn't stopped raining in England since early May.

'Brilliant!' I thought, smiling to myself. 'Maybe we've borrowed their monsoon!'

I stopped smiling when I returned to my hotel. A fresh bowl of fruit sat in my room, and it was swarming with cockroaches. One of the creatures even peered inquisitively at me when I was on the toilet. I rang for help, but the maid who answered my distress call did not understand my predicament. I had to get down on all fours and wave my fingers around my head like antennae before she finally saw the light.

'Ah, *cock-loach* kill!' she announced triumphantly and whipped the offending fruit bowl away into a waiting trolley.

Now I knew why Dr Ratt had been so keen that I eat all those bananas.

Two days later, with all my Thai shopping done, I packed my bags and prepared for the second leg of my journey: India.

I flew into Delhi at 2am, to find it unexpectedly wet and overcast. My mood matched the weather, owing to severe jet-lag, no sleep in twenty hours, and a long wait in the immigration hall before I got my first fag of the day.

India was like a mirror, I decided. Through all the years I had arrived upbeat and well-rested, it had reflected back only good stuff: the humour and kindness of the people, the fascinating street-life, and the vivid, romantic scenery. Now that I was down, I was shown its sordid underbelly. So it was, as I drove into the city, that I was struck by the sheer squalor of the place. The sidewalks were a post-apocalyptic bombsite of open sewer holes, ugly mounds of earth, crumbling temples, and a few struggling shrubs bearing the logo 'Protect our Trees.'

'What a shit-hole!' I thought to myself. 'How can people live like this?'

But live like this they did, for in between all the rubble I could see dark, shadowy figures sleeping on the pavements – beggars, slum dwellers, rickshaw wallahs – as well as all manner of recumbent livestock, from dogs and cows to ponies and pigs. No cats though. They probably had too much sense to walk the streets.

Even as I checked into the Oberoi, even as Anil shook my hand in welcome, I could not shake a gathering sense of gloom. I remembered, for some strange reason, a letter sent me years back from an old friend named Peter, who had castigated me for my lack of pity for India. 'Have you no sense of compassion or outrage at the unimaginable suffering most folk out there have to endure?' he had written. 'When I first returned, I could not eat a meal for weeks without feeling guilty that we should have so much and they so little!'

Peter was right. I knew I was giving work to various tailors and silversmiths in Rajasthan, but was that really enough? I was supposed to be a Buddhist. I was supposed to care for and share with others less fortunate. So what was I doing in a swank four star hotel when most of Delhi was sleeping by the side of the road? It was with a deep sense of shame and disquiet that I finally fell asleep.

I was awoken around 11am by a room-boy with my breakfast: a full English breakfast complete with lashings of eggs, chips, sausages, and fresh filter coffee from a solid silver teapot. But Peter's words still echoed in my mind, and I found I'd lost my appetite.

'No like?' asked the room-boy, waiting for his tip. '*Why* no like?'

To cheer me up, he switched on the brand new TV in my room and rammed the volume up to maximum. Then he proudly rattled off how many channels there were and flicked through them all to show me what to expect, though most of them were blank or had wavy-line static interference. The only crystal clear channel showed a fat, jolly Indian singing to a tree.

'Now come Santa Barbara!' predicted the room-boy, sitting on my bed. 'Next come Nanny and Professor!'

I instantly stopped playing with my food and ushered him out the door. The last thing I needed right now was a teenage TV addict.

Around noon I forced myself from the hotel and out into the dank, stifling heat. I needed to visit the Thomas Cook office at the Imperial Hotel in Janpath so I could change some money. Once there, I loaded up with a heavy bagful of rupees—all stapled up in wads of 50s and 100s—and walked around the corner to Pema's shop at No. 17, the Tibetan Bazar. It occurred to me that I was strolling the street, casually carrying around enough rupees to feed half of Delhi for a week. And that thought triggered off a memory of Spud whipping out a big roll of rupees in the middle of Main Bazar one day, and of the whole street instantly grinding to a halt.

'Put that *away!*' I had hissed at him. 'These people have never seen so much money in their *lives!*'

I felt much better after I gave all my cash to Pema – it wasn't burning a hole in my pockets anymore. I owed Pema big time from the previous trip, and I knew the money was going to poor people, mainly Tibetan refugees, who really needed the work. I also knew—or thought I did—that Pema himself didn't make much from his business. The only luxury he had ever afforded himself, to my knowledge, was his air-conditioning unit, which started blasting frigid air down my neck the moment I entered the shop.

Pema was in good spirits. He had finally, after all these years, got his head around making a profit. I knew this because as soon as I pointed at a bone bracelet I liked, Pema said, 'Actually, the price of this item has gone up.' When asked why, he said, 'Electric city gone, production limited.' I eyed him warily and demanded a further explanation. 'Too many power-cut,' shrugged Pema. 'No work possible in dark, and no work means little production, so they ask more price to make up loss.'

'Well, fair enough,' I thought. 'No bullshit there. Pay the man and shut up.'

Besides, I didn't have much choice. One look around Pema's shop, now packed with other foreign buyers, told me all I needed to know. Pema didn't give a fig whether I bought from him or not.

In Bobby's shop later on, I met a young guy named Christof, who was the main importer of silver into Germany. I told Christof I was having doubts about my business, that I was a Buddhist who had come to India to seek enlightenment, not riches, and I now felt I was exploiting the country, not contributing to it.

'Don't be sorry,' said Christof. 'I come to India to live like a sadhu, and after two years of getting up to meditate at four in the morning and living on three bowls of rice a day, I can tell you one thing for sure: *no one* who comes here for enlightenment has success. Imagine you grew up in the western world and have a completely different culture, education, and belief system. With this, you come to India looking for the spiritual life, and the effort is too much. Even the Indians, who do this all the time, have only one or two per cent success. And those few yogis who have found their way are eager only to continue their personal practice. They have no longing to teach *other* people anything.'

I asked Christof what he had learnt from all his spiritual searching, and he said, 'I learnt that my place is not in the mountains. It is in the world.'

More accurately, he added, it was in the world of silver. He had met a Swiss guy up in the hills who was bringing in jewellery from Thailand and Indonesia, then selling it on to Kashmiris in India. When the Swiss guy's wife got pregnant and they tried to get home from Kashmir, Christof had helped them back to Delhi, braving martial law and nightly curfews in Srinagar, and had been rewarded with ten kilos of high quality silver for his troubles. That was how he'd got started in business.

In two days it would be Gandhi's birthday, Bobby informed us, so all the shops of Paharganj would be shutting down—except for those who paid a five thousand rupee charge to the government for the privilege of staying open.

'Nobody pays five thousand rupees,' Bobby said with a smirk. 'If any policeman check them, they pay him five *hundred* rupees. Much cheaper than five thousand!'

I asked where Babu was. I had brought a couple of extra special 'books' for him from Bangkok, and I was anticipating his delighted grin. But Babu had just got married, said Bobby, and had temporarily lost interest in books. He had been gone the past month, experiencing the real thing.

₹

Chapter 34

The Dark Side of Delhi

It was typical, but the one time I had no expectations of Bobby — no order placed, nothing to wait for or check out — he had a full stock of amazing stone jewellery. It was so amazing, actually, that Christof and I were soon fighting over it. Yes, there we were: two so-called holy men squabbling over baubles, bangles, and beads. And when I said I had no money left, Bobby just smiled and said, 'No problem boss, pay me from UK!'

As Christof and I tottered out afterwards with a big sack of silver apiece, he invited me to share a meal. His restaurant of choice was the 'cheap and best' Khosla Cafe at the bottom of Main Bazar.

'This is where poor people come,' said Christof, 'when all they can afford is a simple meal of dhal, rice, and curd.' It was also, he added, a great place to meet other travellers, since everybody ate together on long communal tables.

The first person we met there was a morphine addict named John.

'You won't believe it, man,' said John. 'But they've got this pharmacy at Delhi airport, right there in the departure lounge, and you can score morphine across the counter. One time I missed a plane home because of that and spent three days crashed out there. Best three days of my life!'

According to Christof, who knew John quite well, this was where he had first acquired his habit. And as dusk drew in, a number of Indians appeared to help him feed it.

'Mister *John!*' they hissed in the darkness. 'Hashish, opium, heroin, what you like?'

Mister John duly disappeared, along with half the cafe's other clientele, only to reappear minutes later with his pockets rustling with little packets. He then began working on his big decision of the day: what kind of lassi to have. Should he have the banana lassi, a lemon lassi, a mango lassi, or simply a plain lassi? The choice was simply staggering. I watched, fascinated, as the moon began to rise and John still had not come to a verdict. Every so often he would turn to us and seriously enquire, 'What do *you* think? I had the banana yesterday. What about the papaya today?' And we would nod sagely, and say, 'Yeah, that's a good idea, man. Go for it!' But then he didn't, just sat there for another hour until his morphine guy turned up and saved him the decision.

'What a sad sack!' I observed. 'The whole day gone and he can't even choose a drink!'

Christof was unruffled. He knew India, he said, and it was full of freaks who only hung out here because the drugs were cheap and readily available. Used-up addicts who lacked even the faintest interest in the country or its people. He only ate here himself, he added, because 'you can see all India passing by from this cafe—a non-stop procession of weddings, funerals, beggars, travellers, pedlars, pilgrims, and animals. It's like an endless Hindi road movie, and the best thing about it is that it doesn't cost one rupee!'

Around 9pm, I trudged back to Bobby's to ask if he could

send my Thai silver back to the UK by courier. I couldn't take it home by hand, because it was sure to be confiscated.

'No problem, boss!' said Bobby brightly, 'but now I am just closing. And there are festivals for next few days, so I go see my family. How much longer are you in India? Another week? Bring me stuff at end, okay?'

It wasn't okay at all, but what other choice did I have? Indian festivals and holidays – they were the ultimate penalty cards in the Indian board game I was playing, and I really should have seen them coming. All the way home, I was kicking myself for leaving the Thai goods in the hotel and not giving them straight to Bobby, but it was too late for lamentation. The dice had been cast, and they had fallen against me.

Back at the Oberoi, I took stock of my situation. I couldn't be sure, but I thought I might be falling out of love with India. Either that, or too many events were conspiring to stop me from enjoying it. I couldn't get my head around going to Jaipur or Pushkar this time since it was too hot, and had resigned myself to a whole week in Delhi, holed up in the Oberoi like some hippy prince in exile.

I made a call home to Madge to cheer myself up, but she couldn't understand my decision. 'You're not going to *Pushkar?*' she exclaimed. 'But you *love* Pushkar!' I told her Gordhan and Satish were coming to Delhi to take my orders in my room, and she couldn't believe that either. 'A whole week in a hotel room?' she asked, sounding horrified. 'And you're dragging those poor people halfway across Rajasthan just to see you?'

I didn't have much choice, I replied. I wasn't staying at the Oberoi because I liked it. I couldn't go outside because of the torrential rains and the 95 per cent humidity. I couldn't go shopping because of the everlasting succession of festivals: first Durga, then Gandhi's birthday, and finally Dussehra. And I couldn't fly home early because I was waiting for Bobby. Also, my airline required a one week minimum stay in India or else I'd have to pay the full, non-discounted fare. In short, being completely out of funds, I was stranded.

With so much time on my hands, I took to reading all the English language newspapers they kept shoving under my door. I also watched a lot of TV. By the third day I was scraping the walls. I knew I was going mad when a room-boy called up to see if I wanted anything, and I said no, I was watching Aerobics Oz-Style on Star Plus.

Seven days was too long to spend in Delhi, I decided. Somehow, sitting in that luxury suite—which most people would have given their right arm for—I was sinking into depression again. Yes, I was in India, but to all intents and purposes I was isolated from it. My tour of Thailand had left me so rundown, so burnt out, that here I was, in my favourite country in the world, and I couldn't get off the bed.

I had lost the Buddhist middle way again. By taking on two countries at once, by obsessing over money and business to the exclusion of all else, I had lost my balance. One step further, and I would descend into an irrevocable tailspin of self-destruction, just like Spud. In the end, that realisation alone was worth the experience. Yes, this long week of lonely confinement had been painful, but it was another important step on my road to recovery.

₹

Chapter 35

Burn Out

My long-awaited visitors arrived on day six. First there was Gordhan, looking hot and glum, and then came Satish, looking even hotter and very sedated. One too many bhang lassis, I surmised. Neither of them had much to say. They just wanted to soak in the air conditioning, take my orders, and go home. Gordhan had met my old friend, Fateh, he reported, and Fateh wasn't happy. His son Ajay had just got back from America and was totally transformed. He now had a crew-cut and a portable stereo, and wore brand name trainers. Most disconcertingly, he had picked up so many ghetto slang expressions that his own parents couldn't understand him. Indu had apparently asked what he thought of the States and he'd replied, 'Well, uh, that's kind of a tough question, man.' So tough indeed that she never got an answer.

Satish was a little more forthcoming. He waited for Gordhan to leave, then asked, 'Why you no come Pushkar? You miss big occasion! You miss brooming of Brahmins!'

Apparently Rajiv Gandhi had not died in vain. One of his main reforms, the right of *harijans* or untouchables to take political office, had finally percolated through to Pushkar. Thus it was that when Pushkar had held the 'open lottery' for the local elections, the name that came out of the hat for the post of Municipal Chairman was not only an untouchable, but a lady road sweeper. The resident Brahmins couldn't believe it. Here was someone whose shadow they would have avoided the day before—since standing in it would have required weeks of self-purification—suddenly elevated to a position to give them orders. Even worse, as the lottery went on, other untouchables were elected onto the same council, making her position quite unassailable. At first, said Satish, she'd kept her broom by her side to hit any Brahmins who might complain. Then she realised she was in power for five long years and needed only the 'broom of government sanction' to sweep aside any opposition. Indeed, since her post entailed control over vital things like lighting and sanitation, the Brahmins had taken to calling her 'Mother Goddess' and kissing her feet. After all, they didn't want tons of garbage unexpectedly dumped on their doorsteps.

Satish had seen George in Pushkar market two days before. 'He lose all his hair, cut it off. Now he look like very poor man. I don't think he can buy *chapati*!' Likely to join him, according to Satish, was my old friend, Ram, who was on the run yet again—this time for passing bad cheques. This news made me despair, and I wished I had never bought Ram his camels all those years before. Money and power seemed to have gone to his head.

Just as Spud's empire had collapsed around him, so too had Ram's. He had acquired Spud's habit of buying on credit and had obtained the lease on a string of handicraft shops in Pushkar by paying the minimum deposit possible—using Eri's money as collateral then failing to pay the balance. Just like Spud, he'd overextended himself. As the bills piled up and people lost trust in him, Ram fled Pushkar forever and hid out in his village.

Unfortunately, that was not the end of Ram's story. Whereas Spud had turned to drugs, Ram had turned to drink. And one fateful day, just as he thought he had successfully evaded his creditors, he took one drink too many and ran his car straight into an oncoming truck. He had survived, but his face had been so disfigured that even Rose, who had rushed him to England for reconstructive surgery, had trouble recognising him. Now he was crippled at both ends, top and bottom, and everyone was agreed on one thing: that Ram's bad karma had finally caught up with him and that it was heaven's justice.

'I wonder whether he wouldn't have been happier staying poor,' I said. 'At least he would have had a few friends.'

'He is now crazy life,' commented Satish. 'Even Rose no speak him.'

'Really?' I exclaimed, shocked. 'Why not?'

This, as it turned out, was the saddest story of all. Poor Rose had learnt that Ram had spawned three children by his village wife, and—this being India—he had never had any intention of leaving them to marry her. She had sacrificed some of the best years of her life, and was now regarded as a whore in the country she loved. All for the love of a two-faced con artist on crutches. I determined that if I ever met Ram again I would treat him like an untouchable and simply turn my back on him.

After Satish left, I began packing my bags, making ready to leave India the following day. As I did so, I came across a single page of an old diary I had written back in 1990, the year I had started doing business. In this diary, which was actually a tape transcript, I was in love with India; I couldn't get enough of it.

255

'Now I'm in the country itself,' I'd enthused. 'Vast, heaving, cacophonic – and the rush of sensations is like being shot full of adrenalin. I just want to write about it, or paint it, or put it to music. I feel energised, buzzed up, ready to explode with the sheer power of it. Two days into Delhi and I'm ready to get on a bus. Any bus to Jaipur will do. Six trippy hours to observe the mad traffic passing by, to get my head back into India, to let a new mass of thoughts and impressions roll in. And then, at the other end, I'll be in another hotel, unpacking my bags, putting up the mosquito net, waiting for the inevitable power-cut, and excitedly recounting the day's events into my tape-recorder by candlelight.'

Those days were over. Ten years on, and I wasn't sure when—or if—I would ever return to India. Maybe it was just a passing phase. I certainly hoped so, but with Ram gone beyond redemption and the Pushkar Posse no longer coming to Pushkar, I felt like a dying breed, the last of the old style Indian traders.

Where were Nick and Anna? Gone back to Canada for good and having their first baby. Where were Susie and Raju? Finally returned to Dagenham, with three kids, and living on social security. And where was Spud? Propping up the door of a Soho nightclub, according to one report, coked up to the eyeballs and begging for tips.

As for me, it seemed like a good time to stop. The Asian markets were running down fast, and the old hippy-dippy fashion in clothing and jewellery was giving way to copy designer stuff which I couldn't legally import. Foreign buyers were now thin on the ground, and those few remaining, like George, were barely hanging on. It felt like the end of an era.

I was so tired of it all, so jaded and world-weary, that a buzzy bus ride to Jaipur was the last thing on my mind. It was all I could do to haul myself into a taxi on my last day in India, and take a short ride down to Paharganj. I was finally going to drop off my Thai silver with Bobby.

But Bobby wasn't there. The shutters of his shop were firmly shut and one of his neighbours told me he had 'gone mountains, too much hot.'

'Well,' I thought wearily, 'that's it. That's the final nail in my coffin. I will now be wandering into Heathrow with twenty-five kilos of counterfeit Thai jewellery plus twenty-five kilos of Indian jewellery—with no receipts, since I'd forgot to ask Bobby for any. So unless Mr Missal is too sick or too lazy to walk over to Terminal 4 on a Sunday, I'm dead in the water.'

And I was too burnt out to care.

*

The scene at Indira Gandhi Airport was chaos. It was a Saturday night, the most popular time to travel, and the whole concourse was a heaving mass of sweating bodies, some of them literally climbing over each other as they tried to find their flights.

I located my own flight, Thai Airways, but there was a problem at check-in. An Indian family at the head of the queue was trying to get a fridge on board as 'hand luggage.' It wasn't a particularly big fridge, but it was obviously not going to fit in an overhead locker. It wasn't even a very good fridge, because they were trying to take it back to London for a replacement.

While all this was going on, a quiet voice behind me said, 'You look stressed, man. Anything wrong?'

I turned round to face a small, bearded hippy wearing a benign smile and studying my anxious, twitching fingers. I hadn't even been aware that my fingers were twitching, I was so much on edge. I could have told him the truth, that I was already dreading English customs, but I put a brave face on instead and said, 'Hate flying. Always have.'

The serene little figure nodded in sympathy and said, 'Yeah, I know what you mean, man. Here, have some of these. You'll sleep like a baby!' With that, he stuffed a strip of ten white tablets into my hand and told me to take two whenever I felt nervous.

That was the start of the flight from hell. It started out okay – I had quiet people sitting next to me and no reason to complain. But then the lights went out, and my insomnia kicked in. With seven hours to go and nothing to do but worry about Mr Missal, I panicked. I took out the plastic strip and popped two pills. An hour went by and nothing happened, so I took a couple more. Round about 3am, when everybody else was sound asleep and I was still on full alert, I thought, "sod it," and downed the whole packet.

'What's the worst that can happen?' I reasoned. 'I'll get into Heathrow massively sedated and won't give a shit what they do to me!'

The first sign of trouble came when I tried to go to the toilet but couldn't. My legs had turned to rubber, and I couldn't get out of my seat. At the same time I could feel an awful rumbling in my stomach, and I knew I was going to be sick. Very sick.

I managed to get to my feet, then lurched down to the back of the plane, waking up a number of passengers as I did so, and stuck my head down a toilet. I retched and retched and retched until I was quite sure my guts were empty, but no, there I went again. My head stayed down that toilet until touchdown. At some point, the only medically trained stewardess on board fished the empty strip out of my pocket and informed me I had just overdosed on morphine.

'Oh, that explains it,' I gurgled miserably. 'I'm allergic to opiates.'

Just when I thought I was going to die, that the nightmare would never end, I was carried to the front of the plane, put into a wheelchair, and gently pushed—with two suitcases of contraband silver on my lap—into the customs hall.

Tony saw me coming and jumped back in shock. 'My God, Frank!' he declared. 'You look white as a sheet!'

Mr Missal, who was standing right behind him, was not so sympathetic. 'Oh, now he has a *wheelchair,*' he sighed dismissively. 'You think I am believing *this?*'

Without further ado, he plunged into my rucksack and pulled out, of all things, my Buddhist prayer bag. For some reason he was sure I was hiding illicit receipts in there. But in amongst a thick wad of religious guidance notes I hardly ever looked at, he found something entirely different: a small paper packet of brown powder I had never seen before, cunningly taped to the back of a photograph of my mother. On it was written the single spidery word: 'Smack'.

It was Spud's final act of revenge, a really evil one. I could only assume he'd planted this 'heroin surprise' when he'd posted the prayer bag back to me in '98. As I sat in front of Mr Missal, sick as a dog, I reflected that I had been carrying this tiny time-bomb around for over three years! Had it turned up in India—or even worse in Thailand—I would have been facing a death sentence or at least twenty-five years in jail.

By his expression, I could tell even Mr Missal was stunned by his discovery. All thoughts of silver penalties fled his mind as he calculated the prospect of a quick and immediate promotion. Here at last was a real criminal, one he could really take to town! He opened his mouth to pronounce awful judgement ... but just as he did so, I lurched helplessly forward and projectile-vomited all over him. His entire starched-white uniform was soiled, top to toe, and the offending packet of brown powder flew across the concourse and disappeared into the ether.

'Looks like chicken curry,' Tony observed helpfully. 'Isn't that against your religion?'

'Get him out of here!' Mr Missal howled. 'I am good Brahmin! I do not deserve such treatment! He has made me unclean!'

Tony wheeled me quickly out of the hall and into the bright light of day. 'Well,' he said chirpily. 'That's one way of not paying any duty!'

I didn't quite share the joke. I still felt sicker than I ever had at any time in my life. But as Tony drove me home in his car, I realised how lucky I had been.

And surprise, surprise. I was back in business.

*

Spud's final action – his heroin 'surprise' – didn't go down well. I had faced the death penalty in Asia once before, for falling asleep in the back of a bus going into Malaysia and then trying to get back out again with an unstamped passport. Charged with illegal immigration, I still remembered the terror of sitting in a cell with a noose hanging off the ceiling, waiting to be rescued. I had been, but only when my Thai bus-driver had chanced by and identified me.

This time, there would have been no such lucky escape. Spud, who had once saved my life, had come close to ending it. And after everything else – all the death-threats, the abuse, the tax scams, and the general persecution – this was just a bit too much.

'What a complete and utter bastard!' I fretted a few days later as I recovered. 'He must have planned that years ago!'

But if I was contemplating revenge, I was saved the trouble. Word soon trickled through that Lou, Spud's ex-wife, had taken half his house, and the Inland Revenue had the other half. As for Spud himself, coked and stroked, he was already dead.

Or so I thought.

₹

Postscript

20th October 2012

When Sharon rang that fateful day last Summer, I couldn't believe it. My bald nemesis, who I had thought dead for ten years, had resurfaced – very much alive! And he had not so much returned from the grave, he had never actually been in it! To top it all off, someone had told him I was writing a book about him, and he was gunning for me once again.

What was I to do?

The first thing I did was close my business. I had to. Wherever I went Spud was just one step behind me, asking all my shops where was I, had they seen me lately? It was only a matter of time before one of them cracked and spilled the beans.

The second thing I did was talk to Madge. If I went ahead with this book, I was afraid she might someday be blown up in her sleep. 'It's not enough this time,' I told her, 'to change my name, my passport, my driving licence and my entire appearance. I may have to leave the country!'

But I needn't have worried. The phone rang again this morning, and this time it wasn't Sharon. It was Spud.

'I've read a bit of your book now,' said the familiar menacing voice down the airwaves. 'And it's bollocks.'

'Bollocks?' I stuttered, my mind going into freefall. 'Don't you like it, then?'

'Like it? I love it! It's my *kind* of bollocks.'

'But I have you down as a dangerous, drug-addled, control-freak psychopath!'

'Yeah, I know. But you're forgetting one thing.'

'Oh, what's that?'

Spud gave a low chuckle.

'I always wanted to be famous.'

~ THE END ~

Hi folks, Frank here!

Thank you so much for reading my book, I do hope you enjoyed it! If you did, I would be extremely grateful if you could leave a few words on Amazon as a review: http://authl.it/vy_ Not only are reviews crucial in getting an author's work noticed, but I personally love reviews and treasure them all…even the slightly stinky ones! Oh, and if you *really* enjoyed this book, then maybe you'd like the two prequels, 'Kevin and I in India' http://authl.it/274 and 'Off the Beaten Track: My Crazy Year in Asia' http://authl.it/21z They're more of my madcap adventures in Asia!

P.S. If you like, you can find me on Twitter:
https://twitter.com/Wussyboy

Or catch me on Facebook:
https://www.facebook.com/frank.kusy.5?ref=tn_tnmn

Or if you get the urge, you can always email me:
sparky-frank@hotmail.co.uk

Frank Kusy

Acknowledgements

My sincere gratitude goes to the following people: Terry Murphy (for editing and laughs), Roman Laskowski (for meticulous formatting, web admin and laughs), Anna Donovan (for my lovely cover), Brenda Donovan (for editing my first drafts), Elke Browne (for early encouragement and edits), Cherry Gregory (for the final beta read), Judy Adams (for editing and steadfast support), Nick Kenrick (for pics and tricks), Anna Norris (for lizard hugs), Julie Shaw (for believing in this book like no other), Writing Wildly (for a top pro-edit), and all my friends on Authonomy for all their lovely (and not so lovely!) comments. You have all helped bring the work of my heart to life.

A special mention to my wife, Margreet, for living the dream with me and being the best part of it.

Frank Kusy

About the author

FRANK KUSY is a professional travel writer with nearly thirty years experience in the field. He has written guides to India, Thailand, Burma, Malaysia, Singapore and Indonesia. Of his first work, the travelogue *Kevin and I in India* (1986), the Mail on Sunday wrote: 'This book rings so true of India that most of us will be glad we don't have to go there.'

Born in England (of Polish-Hungarian parents), Frank left Cardiff University for a career in journalism and worked for a while at the Financial Times. India is his first love, the only country he knows which improves on repeated viewings. He still visits for business and for pleasure at least once a year. He lives in Surrey, England, with his wife Margreet and his little cat Sparky.

GRINNING BANDIT BOOKS

A word from our sponsors…

If you enjoyed *Rupee Millionaires*, please check out these other brilliant books:

Kevin and I in India, Off the Beaten Track: My Crazy Year in Asia, Ginger the Gangster Cat, Ginger the Buddha Cat – all by Frank Kusy (Grinning Bandit Books).

Weekend in Weighton by Terry Murphy (Grinning Bandit Books).

The Ultimate Inferior Beings by Mark Roman (Cogwheel Press).

Scrapyard Blues by Derryl Flynn (Grinning Bandit Books)

www.ingramcontent.com/pod-product-compliance
Lightning Source LLC
Chambersburg PA
CBHW060230050426
42448CB00009B/1370